Constitutional and Administrative Law

Visit the *Law Express Series* Companion Website at
www.pearsoned.co.uk/ and find valuable **student**
learning material including

▌ A Study Plan test to assess how well you know the subject
before you begin your revision
▌ Interactive quizzes to test your knowledge of the main points
from each chapter of the book
▌ Further examination questions and guidelines for answering
them
▌ Interactive flashcards to help you revise the main terms and
cases
▌ Printable versions of the topic maps and checklists

Constitutional and Administrative Law

Chris Taylor

PEARSON

Longman

Harlow, England • London • New York • Boston • San Francisco • Toronto • Sydney • Singapore • Hong Kong
Tokyo • Seoul • Taipei • New Delhi • Cape Town • Madrid • Mexico City • Amsterdam • Munich • Paris • Milan

Pearson Education Limited
Edinburgh Gate
Harlow
Essex CM20 2JE
England

and Associated Companies throughout the world
Visit us on the World Wide Web at:
www.pearsoned.co.uk

First published 2008

© Pearson Education Limited 2008

ISBN: 978-1-4058-2191-9

British Library Cataloguing-in-Publication Data
A catalogue record for this book is available from the British Library

Library of Congress Cataloging-in-Publication Data
Taylor, Christopher W.
  Consitutional and administrative law / Chris Taylor.
    p. com.
  Includes bibliographical references and index.
  ISBN 978-1-4058-2191-9 (pbk.)
1. Constitutional law--Great Britain. 2. Adminstrative law--Great Britain. I. Title.
  KD3989.T39 2008
  342.41--dc22   2007036917

10 9 8 7 6 5 4 3 2 1
11 10 09 08 07
Typeset by 3 in 10pt Helvetic Condensed
Printed and bound by Henry Ling Ltd., at the Dorset Press, Dorchester, Dorset

The publisher's policy is to use paper manufactured from sustainable forests.

Contents

Acknowledgements

Our thanks go to all reviewers who contributed to the development of this text, including students who participated in research and focus groups which helped to shape the series format.

Introduction

Constitutional and administrative law is one of the core subjects required for a qualifying law degree and so is a compulsory part of undergraduate law programmes and graduate diploma in law programmes. It is, however, very different from many of the other core legal subjects because it concentrates less on legal rules than on the operation of the system itself – in particular, the operation of the state and the relationship between the state and the individual.

Constitutional law is often described as being where law meets politics and there are frequent references to the political process which directly influences the law which is introduced. Much of the law we work with originates in Parliament in the form of statute and so we must understand how Parliament works and how such statutes are produced. Similarly, in order to appreciate the role played by the common law, we must understand the position of the courts within the constitution. More importantly, constitutional law considers how power is exercised by the state and how those in power are held accountable. This includes the protection of civil liberties and mechanisms for the individual to challenge the exercise of state power.

It is not uncommon to approach constitutional law for the first time with a certain amount of uncertainty, especially if politics is not your favourite subject, but don't worry. Almost all students find themselves enjoying the subject more than they expected and your knowledge of how 'the system' works will be invaluable in your other legal studies. The most important thing to remember is that, because we do not have a written constitution, there is no central set of rules which dictates how the state should operate. Instead, our constitutional system is a web of principles and customs which often appear outdated and vague, so this subject can seem disjointed when compared with other areas of law, but don't assume that it is just you who doesn't understand at first – just remember the basic principles and take a little time to think about *why* the constitution has evolved into the system we have today.

Remember that this is a revision guide, not a core text, so it can never provide you with the depth of understanding which you will need to excel in examinations and it will be no substitute for structured reading around the various topics. What it can do, however, is to focus your revision on the key areas and highlight those additional points which examiners are looking for. The single most common failing in constitutional law examinations is that students write 'common sense' answers, without sufficient reference to the cases and legal principles. We all know (or think we know) what government or Parliament are, but that is not enough – as in any other area of legal writing, you need to produce logical, reasoned arguments supported by relevant authorities if you are to achieve the highest grades.

Guided tour

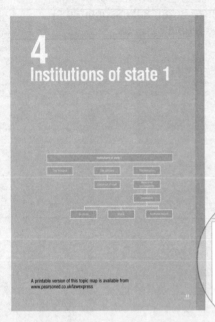

Topic maps – Highlight the main points and allow you to find your way quickly and easily through each chapter.

Revision checklist – How well do you know each topic? Don't panic if you don't know them all, the chapters will help you revise each point so that you will be fully prepared for your exams.

Sample questions – Prepare for what you will be faced with in your exams! Guidance on structuring strong answers is provided at the end of the chapter.

Sample question

Could you answer this question? Below is a typical problem question that could arise on this topic. Guidelines on answering the question are included at the end of this chapter, whilst a sample essay question and guidance on tackling it can be found on the companion website.

Key definition boxes – Make sure you understand essential legal terms.

KEY DEFINITIONS

Federal constitution. A constitution which has a division of powers between the central government and the government of individual states or regions.

Unitary constitution. A constitution with power concentrated in central government. Local government may exist but not with the constitutional status of the states under a federal constitution.

Problem area boxes – Highlight areas where students most often trip up in exams. Use them to make sure you do not make the same mistakes.

The distinction between 'rights' and 'freedoms' has been an important one. Examiners will credit an understanding of the distinction between the two and the different legal implications of each. In this way, be sure to emphasise the difference between a 'right', which can be claimed, and a 'freedom', which exists only until the state removes it.

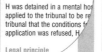

VIL LIBERTIES A

KEY CASE

R (on the application of **Review Tribunal [2001] Q**

Concerning: compatibility of **Human Rights**

Facts

H was detained in a mental ho applied to the tribunal to be re tribunal that the conditions f application was refused, H

Legal principle

Key case and key statutes boxes – Identify the essential cases and statutes that you need to know for your exams.

KEY STATUTES

Human Rights Act 1998, section 6(1)

It is unlawful for a public authority to act in a way w a Convention right.

Further thinking boxes – Illustrate areas of academic debate, and point you towards that extra reading required for the top grades.

FURTHER THINKING

The wording of the caution emphasises that a suspect who does not mention information when questioned, but who later seeks to rely on that information as part of their defence in court may find the court drawing an 'adverse inference' from their failure to provide the information earlier (i.e. concluding that they are lying). This undermines the 'right to silence', which was seen as a fundamental right of the accused and was introduced by the Criminal Justice and Public Order Act 1994. This change was highly criticised and continues to cause argument and concern. See Leng (2001).

Glossary – Forgotten the meaning of a word? Where a word is highlighted in the text, turn to the glossary at the back of the book to remind yourself of its meaning.

Glossary of terms

The glossary is divided into two parts: **key definitions** and **other useful terms**.

The **key definitions** can be found within relevant chapters as well as at the end c book. These are the essential terms that you must know and understand in orde prepare for an examination or a piece of coursework.

The **other useful terms** provide definitions of other terms and phrases which yo encounter in this subject and may have forgotten the meaning of. These terms a highlighted in the text as they occur but the definition can only be found here.

Exam tips – Want to impress examiners? These indicate how you can improve your exam performance and your chances of getting top marks.

EXAM TIP

Make sure to point out that many written constitutions are produced after a revolution, where the citizens rise up against what they see as an oppressive state. In this way the US constitution was written after the War of Independence from Britain and the French constitution was produced after the French Revolution. You can also make the point that, although most countries have a written constitution, the UK is not the only country without such a document. Both New Zealand and Israel also have unwritten constitutions.

Revision notes – Highlight points that you should be aware of in other topic areas, or where your course may adopt a specific approach that you should check with your course tutor before reading further.

REVISION NOTE

Any discussion of the role of judicial review allows you to introduce references to a number of different aspects of constitutional law. For example, as judicial review is a mechanism for the judiciary to exert control over the executive, it can be viewed as part of the 'separation of powers'. Similarly, as judicial review is limited to secondary legislation (which is not debated in Parliament), it can be seen to provide a safeguard to ensure that such delegated powers are not misused.

Table of cases and statutes

Cases

Statutes

1
The constitution of the UK

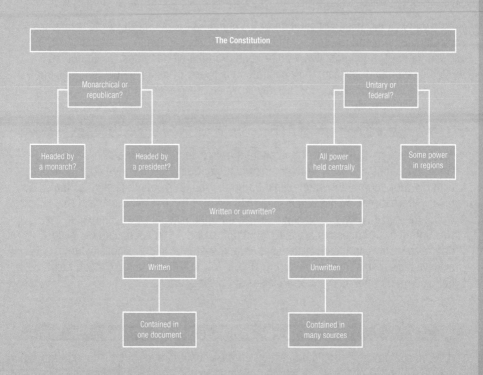

A printable version of this topic map is available from
www.pearsoned.co.uk/lawexpress

Revision Checklist

What you need to know:

☐ What is meant by the term 'constitution'
☐ The difference between a written and an unwritten constitution
☐ The characteristics of both types of constitution
☐ The advantages and disadvantages of written and unwritten constitutions.

Introduction

What is a constitution anyway?

Before you can discuss the operation of the constitution, you need to know what we mean by the term and the answer to this is not as easy as it might first appear. The UK is different from almost every other country in the world in that we do not have a written constitution. Instead, our constitution is a web of mainly unwritten rules and this has serious implications for the way in which 'the system' works.

Essay question advice

Essay questions on the unwritten constitution are an old favourite of examiners. Often, questions will ask you to compare and contrast our unwritten constitution with the more common written constitution (as found in countries such as the USA). Alternatively, an essay question may ask you to consider the extent to which the constitution provides protection for an individual's civil liberties in the UK. Both types of question are fairly straightforward if you appreciate the main differences between the unwritten and written systems, and it is possible to achieve high marks by making sure that you not only describe the constitution but also offer some analysis or criticism of how it operates.

Problem question advice

It is unusual to see a problem question on the constitution as such, although the way in which the unwritten constitution influences the operation of the state can be mentioned in almost any public law question. More likely is a question which may be posed as a scenario but which is, in reality, more of an essay question (see example).

Sample question

Could you answer this question? Below is a typical essay question that could arise on this topic. Guidelines on answering the question are included at the end of this chapter, whilst a sample problem question and guidance on tackling it can be found on the companion website.

'The fact that the UK does not have a written constitution is of no practical significance to the individual.' Discuss

■ What is a constitution?

A 'constitution' simply means a system of rules. Many organisations and clubs have constitutions which set out how people are appointed to run the club and the rules which affect the club's members. In the same way, the constitution of a country sets out how power is held by the state and how that power relates to the citizen. In this way, the constitution can be said to define both a *horizontal* relationship (between the various institutions of state) and a *vertical* relationship (between the state and the individual).

KEY DEFINITION

Constitution. The framework of rules which dictate the way in which power is divided between the various parts of the state and the relationship between the state and the individual.

The state			
The Queen	The executive (government)	Parliament	The judiciary

The individual

In most other countries, this system of rules is contained in a single document which is called 'the constitution' and this illustrates that there are two ways in which the term 'constitution' can be interpreted: first, as a system of rules; and, second, as a piece of paper which sets out that system of rules. This is an important distinction when comparing the unwritten constitution of the UK with other countries (such as the USA) which have a written constitution.

When answering questions, make the distinction between the constitution as an 'abstract' term (i.e. a set of rules) and the 'concrete' constitution (an actual document which contains those rules).

■ Types of constitution

Before considering the differences between the unwritten constitution of the UK and the written constitutions of most other countries, it is also possible to identify other ways in which constitutions can be classified:

Monarchical and republican constitutions

Under a 'monarchical' constitution, the head of state is a King or Queen and state powers are exercised in their name. In this way, although the majority of power in the UK now resides with Parliament and the government, the Queen remains the head of state.

By contrast, a 'republican' constitution has as its head of state a president, who has far more power than the current Queen. Such powers are justified on the basis that the president is elected and so accountable to the people, unlike a monarch, who is head of state simply by birth.

KEY DEFINITIONS

Monarchical constitution. A constitution based on the historical power of a monarch who acts as head of state and in whose name power is exercised by the government.

Republican constitution. A constitution with an elected president as the head of state who exercises power in the name of the state.

Federal and unitary constitutions

In some countries, state powers are divided into those exercised by central government and those exercised by the states or regions. This results in a 'federal' constitution.

For example, in the USA, central government (also known as the 'federal' government) retains the most important powers relating to matters such as defence, whereas the individual 'states' have powers on a local level and have their own constitutional status.

By contrast, the UK has a 'unitary' constitution where all power resides in the central state institutions. We do have local government, in the form of local councils, but these can be altered (or even abolished) by the central government at any time.

KEY DEFINITIONS

Federal constitution. A constitution which has a division of powers between the central government and the government of individual states or regions.

Unitary constitution. A constitution with power concentrated in central government. Local government may exist but not with the constitutional status of the states under a federal constitution.

EXAM TIP

Examiners will expect to see a discussion of the differences between written and unwritten constitutions. It is less common for students to mention the other ways in which constitutions may be categorised and so mentioning these will make your answer stand out from the crowd. You could include the example of the abolition of the Greater London Council by the government in 1985 as an example of the power remaining with central government under a unitary constitution (the federal government of the USA could not abolish one of the states in this way under the federal system) and you could also discuss whether it is preferable to have an elected president, under a republican constitution, or an unelected monarch, as in the UK.

■ Written and unwritten constitutions

The most important way to classify constitutions is between 'written' and 'unwritten'.

Written constitutions

As has already been mentioned, almost every country apart from the UK has a written constitution, which contains the main rules governing the power of the state and the relationship between the state and the individual in a single document. For the citizens of the country, the constitution is an enormously important document because it prevents the state from abusing its powers and safeguards the rights of the individual.

Key provisions of the Constitution of the United States of America
Article 1 – establishes the first branch of government – the legislature.
Article 2 – establishes the second branch of government – the executive.
Article 3 – establishes the third branch of government – the judiciary.
Article 4 – provides that all states must honour the laws of the other states.
Article 5 – outlines the procedure for amending the Constitution.

Changing the written constitution

In order to protect the citizen against the state, the constitution has to be strong (otherwise the government will simply change it) but, if it is too strong, then it cannot be amended to reflect changes in society. For example, the original US constitution included the right to own slaves, which was later removed when the majority recognised this as unacceptable.

EXAM TIP

Make sure to point out that many written constitutions are produced after a revolution, where the citizens rise up against what they see as an oppressive state. In this way the US constitution was written after the War of Independence from Britain and the French constitution was produced after the French Revolution. You can also make the point that, although most countries have a written constitution, the UK is not the only country without such a document. Both New Zealand and Israel also have unwritten constitutions.

Unwritten constitutions

By contrast, countries such as the UK with an unwritten constitution have no single document which sets out power relationships within the state. Instead, we have many sources, both written and unwritten, which combine to provide the rules regulating the state. These sources are discussed in the next chapter.

REVISION NOTE

The unwritten constitution can be brought into every topic within constitutional and administrative law. For example, examiners will frequently set questions on specific sources of the constitution, such as royal prerogative or constitutional conventions, but always remember to discuss these in the context of the unwritten constitution and emphasise that you understand that such sources are important because they operate as part of the unwritten system. Examiners will give you credit for making such connections between different parts of the syllabus.

Rights and the constitution

One of the most important aspects of a written constitution is that it provides protection for individual rights. For example, the US constitution specifically lists a number of rights as amendments to the constitution (e.g. the First Amendment – the right to freedom of speech). Such rights cannot be taken away by the state. Under an unwritten constitution, the state can take away individual rights at any time because they are not protected by the constitution.

EXAM TIP

In considering the status of individual rights in the UK, remember that, although the unwritten constitution does not protect rights, we now have the European Convention on Human Rights, as implemented by the Human Rights Act 1998, which does provide greater protection for certain rights.

Characteristics of written and unwritten constitutions

Almost all exam questions on the unwritten constitution will ask you to outline the key characteristics of both written and unwritten constitutions and to compare their strengths and weaknesses. This type of comparison demonstrates the analytical skills which examiners want to see in answers.

| Written constitutions | |
Advantages	Disadvantages
All key provisions are contained in a single document.	Requires one document to encompass the regulation of the entire constitution.
Provides a clear statement of how the state should operate with no uncertainty over words. Everyone can read and agree what it says.	May lead to litigation over the precise meanings of the terms used, particularly if the language is outdated.
Protects the individual from abuses by the government of the day.	May be difficult to amend if the provisions become outdated (e.g. the USA and slavery).
Provides clear protection of individual rights.	May be inflexible and unresponsive to change.

Unwritten constitutions	
Advantages	Disadvantages
Flexible and responsive to changing circumstances.	Can appear vague and uncertain. No single agreed source of constitutional law.
Leaves the state free to develop the law for the benefit of citizens.	Leaves the state free to abuse its powers and develop laws which act against its citizens.
Encourages the evolution of the constitution.	Provides no protection for individual civil liberties.

Chapter Summary:
Putting it all together

TEST YOURSELF

☐ Can you tick all the points from the revision checklist at the beginning of this chapter?

☐ Take the **end-of-chapter quiz** on the companion website.

☐ Test your knowledge of the cases below with the **revision flashcards** on the website.

☐ Attempt the essay question from the beginning of the chapter using the guidelines below.

☐ Go to the companion website to try out other questions.

Answer guidelines

See the essay question at the start of the chapter.

Points to remember when answering this question

▌ Clearly define what is meant by a 'constitution'.

▌ Recognise the two key relationships which are defined by the constitution: between the organs of the state and between the state and the individual.

▌ Set out the key characteristics of the UK constitution as monarchical (rather than republican) and unitary (rather than federal).

▌ Work through the advantages and disadvantages of the written and unwritten constitutions listed above.

▮ It could be argued that our constitution appears to work reasonably well because we are a prosperous society with relative freedom.

▮ But you can also consider the negligible protection for individual rights provided by the UK constitution. Because the state is not constrained by a written constitution, it can change the law and remove our rights.

▮ You could conclude that the constitution of the UK has worked well but that, if something does go wrong, there is little protection for the individual to be found in the constitution.

Make your answer really stand out

▮ Remember to read the question carefully. Is it asking you to list the characteristics of the constitution or (as in this question) assess the impact on the individual citizen?

▮ Do not simply divide constitutions between written and unwritten but also consider the other ways in which constitutions can be defined (federal/unitary; monarchical/ republican). Most students only mention written/unwritten, so this additional discussion will earn extra credit.

▮ Note that the question does not simply require description (what the constitution is) but also analysis (how well it works). Students always do well on description but fall down on analysis. For this reason, the best way to increase your overall mark is to demonstrate that you can weigh up the advantages and disadvantages.

▮ Always draw your arguments together into a proper conclusion which expresses a view on the central question and which is based on the points which you have raised in your answer.

FURTHER READING

Bogdanor, V. (ed.) (2003) *The British Constitution in the Twentieth Century*. Oxford: OUP.

Bogdanor, V. (2004) 'Our New Constitution', 120 *Law Quarterly Review* 242–62.

Elliott, M. (2007) 'Bicameralism, Sovereignty and the Unwritten Constitution', 5 *International Journal of Constitutional Law* 370.

Goldsworthy, J. (2003) 'Homogenizing Constitutions', 23 *Oxford Journal of Legal Studies* 483.

Juss, S. S. (2006) 'Constitutionalising Rights without a Constitution: The British Experience under Article 6 of the Human Rights Act 1998', 27 *Statute Law Review* 29.

Kay, R. S. 'Substance and Structure as Constitutional Protections: Centennial Comparisons', *Public Law* 428–39.

Sedley, S. (1994) 'The Sound of Silence: Constitutional Law Without a Constitution', 110 *Law Quarterly Review* 270–91.

Walker, N. (2000) 'Beyond the Unitary Conception of the United Kingdom Constitution', *Public Law* 384–404.

2
Where does the constitution come from?

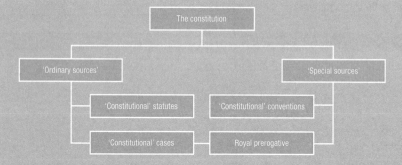

A printable version of this topic map is available from
www.pearsoned.co.uk/lawexpress

Revision Checklist

What you need to know:

☐ The way in which the unwritten constitution has a number of interrelated sources.

☐ The operation of 'ordinary sources', statute and common law, which exist in other areas of law.

☐ The operation of 'special sources', constitutional conventions and royal prerogative, which apply only to constitutional and administrative law.

☐ The distinctive features of the 'special sources'.

Introduction

The state operates in accordance with rules but, to apply the rules, it is first necessary to understand where they come from.

One of the problems with an unwritten constitution is that there is no single document which sets out how the state works and where the power lies. Instead, this information comes from a number of different sources. This area is relatively straightforward but, in answering exam questions, it is important to show that you understand the differences between the various sources and how they work together. Examiners usually concentrate on the 'special' sources when setting questions, but be aware that you may find references to constitutional sources in questions on other topics, such as parliamentary sovereignty or separation of powers.

Essay question advice

Essay questions on the sources of constitutional law provide an excellent opportunity for the well-prepared student to demonstrate their knowledge and here the most important point to remember is the distinction between the 'ordinary' and 'special' sources and the ways in which constitutional conventions and royal prerogative are very different from statute and common law. It is more common, however, for examiners to concentrate on the 'special' sources and set a more detailed question on the operation of either constitutional conventions and royal prerogative. Here, the examiner will be looking for both a clear statement of the characteristics of the source and, in particular, their status as 'non-legal' rules. Also remember that the better answer will always include a number of examples.

Problem question advice

The topic of sources does not lend itself easily to problem questions but an imaginative examiner may seek to test students with a series of scenarios, each illustrating one of the sources. More likely is a problem which concentrates on either constitutional conventions or royal prerogative and, here, the key issue will be the difficulties in enforcing such rules through the courts. Once again, the use of examples is crucial to achieving a high mark.

Sample question

Could you answer this question? Below is a typical essay question that could arise on this topic. Guidelines on answering the question are included at the end of this chapter, whilst a sample problem question and guidance on tackling it can be found on the companion website.

ESSAY QUESTION

The constitution of England and Wales is to be found, not in a single document, but in a range of sources. Discuss.

■ Sources of the constitution

One of the key differences between the UK and a country with a written constitution is that we cannot look to a single document to explain how the state operates. Instead, we must consider a variety of sources which provide the rules governing how the state should operate. It is important to realise that, because there is no central 'blueprint' for how the state works (in the form of a written constitution), there is nothing to prevent these various rules from coming into conflict and this does occur. As a result, this can be a confusing area to study. However, it is not as difficult as it may first appear, providing that you approach the various sources in turn, taking some time to understand the differences between them.

■ Ordinary sources

In considering the sources of the constitution, it is possible to make a distinction between what are sometimes termed 'ordinary' and 'special' sources. This simply means that some constitutional sources are viewed as 'ordinary' because they also apply in other areas of law, whereas the 'special' sources are to be found only in the study of constitutional and administrative law. Because the ordinary sources are more familiar, it is advisable to begin with those.

Statute

Perhaps the most familiar source of law is statute and, as with every other area of law, there are many Acts of Parliament which impact on the operation of the constitution. Such Acts may set out specific powers of the state or, alternatively, provide protections for the citizen.

EXAM TIP

Although the constitution of the UK is 'unwritten', the existence of 'constitutional' statutes means that there are a large number of sources of constitutional law which are, indeed, written. Rather that simply stating that 'the UK has an unwritten constitution', point out that there are written sources which impact upon the operation of the constitution but what is lacking is a *single* document setting out the powers of the state. Also, emphasise that, over time, many of the 'special' sources have been replaced by statutory powers in order to make them more accountable to Parliament and the courts.

Identifying a 'constitutional' statute

Although many statutes have a constitutional significance, they are not always easy to identify. This is because, unlike other areas of law, the title of the Act does not provide a clear indication of its relevance. For example, whereas it is clear that the Unfair Contract Terms Act 1977 has something to do with the law of contract and that the Theft Act 1968 relates to the criminal offence of theft, it is rare for an Act of Parliament to contain a reference to the constitution in its title. For this reason, we must look elsewhere in order to identify a 'constitutional' statute.

The key to deciding which statutes are 'constitutional' is to ask: 'does the Act impact on either the workings of the state or on the relationship between the state and the individual?' In this way, we look not at the name of the statute but to its effects.

Some 'constitutional' statutes

Act of Union with Scotland 1707

United England and Scotland, giving power to the Westminster Parliament to legislate over Scotland.

Bill of Rights 1689

Established Parliament (rather than the monarch) as the supreme law-making body in England. Restricted the powers of the King and set out basic individual rights.

Parliament Acts 1911 and 1949

Removed the ability of the House of Lords to reject legislation which has been passed by the House of Commons, leaving only the power to delay Bills for a fixed period of time.

His Majesty's Declaration of Abdication Act 1936

Allowed King Edward VIII to give up the throne in order to marry American divorcee Wallis Simpson.

Human Rights Act 1998

Made domestic courts 'courts of human rights' by providing direct access to many of the rights contained in the European Convention on Human Rights. Placed a statutory obligation on the state to act in accordance with the Convention rights.

House of Lords Act 1999

Removed the rights of the majority of hereditary peers to sit and vote in the House of Lords.

Common law

The second of our 'ordinary sources' of constitutional law is the common law and there are many judicial decisions which impact on the working of the constitution. As with statute, the difficulty is in establishing precisely which cases have this effect and, once again, the best way of approaching any discussion is by reference to example. You should always include a number of such authorities to support your arguments.

EXAM TIP

When discussing the role of the common law within the constitution, point out that there are constitutional issues where the courts seek to restrict the powers of the state. Such conflicts highlight the constitutional importance of an independent judiciary as part of the 'separation of powers' (see Chapter 4).

KEY CASE

Entick v. *Carrington* (1765) 19 State Tr 1029

Facts

The King's messengers broke into Entick's house on orders from the Secretary of State to seize both Entick and his papers (he was suspected of treason). Entick challenged the legality of the search but the Secretary of State argued that such powers were an essential part of government.

Legal principle

The state had to act within legal authority. Therefore, if there was no statute or common law precedent which authorised the search, it would be illegal. The state was not above the law.

KEY CASE

Duport Steel Ltd and others v. *Sirs and others* [1980] 1 All ER 529

Concerning: the relationship between Parliament and the courts

Facts

A union called a strike of its members. The court was required to decide whether the union's actions were 'in furtherance of a trade dispute', as required by the relevant Act of Parliament.

Legal principle

Sets out the relationship between Parliament and the courts. As stated by Lord Diplock, 'Parliament makes the laws, the judiciary interpret them'.

Congreve v. *Home Office* **[1976] QB 629**

Concerning: the powers of the Executive

Facts

The government decided to raise the cost of a TV licence but, after the planned increase was announced, a number of people bought new licences at the old price before the increase came into effect. In order to recover the money lost, the government decided to revoke the licences unless the increased fee was paid.

Legal principle

The actions proposed by the government amounted to a tax which had not been authorised by Parliament. The government could only levy taxes on the public where Parliament had expressly authorised them to do so.

REVISION NOTE

Discussion of the common law as a source of constitutional law raises issues of parliamentary sovereignty and the separation of powers (Chapter 4). In looking at both of these topics, you will see that, although the courts must follow the will of Parliament, they are able to challenge wrongdoing on the part of the Executive.

As you can see, statute and common law act as sources of constitutional law, much as they do in other areas of law. For this reason, the key to a good answer is to include examples, such as those above, to illustrate the ways in which Parliament and the courts have shaped the rules of the constitution. You should also emphasise the clarity and certainty of statute and common law when compared with the 'special' sources.

Special sources

Having considered the 'ordinary' sources of statute and common law, we must now examine those sources of law which are particular to constitutional and administrative law. Unlike their more familiar counterparts, these sources do not appear in other legal subjects and so they can, initially, appear confusing. The key to understanding how they operate is to recognise that their origins lie, not in Parliament, but in the history of England.

Royal prerogative

There remain a number of important powers within the constitution which fall under the title 'Royal prerogative' or 'prerogative powers' and which have their origins in the powers originally exercised by the monarch. Although Parliament is now the most powerful of the institutions of state, the Executive can still exercise a number of powers without the consent of either Parliament or the courts and this absence of accountability makes such powers particularly useful to government.

KEY DEFINITION

Royal prerogative. This was defined by Dicey as 'the residue of discretionary or arbitrary authority . . . legally left in the Hands of the Crown . . . the remaining portion of the Crown's original authority' (see Dicey (1885)).

It is possible to divide such powers into those relating to foreign affairs and those relating to domestic affairs. It is also possible to make a distinction between those powers which are exercised by the monarch and those which are exercised by the government.

Problem area

Be clear on the use of the term 'the Crown'. This does not just mean the Queen but also means the government which acts 'in the name of the Crown'.

EXAMPLE: 'FOREIGN' PREROGATIVES

Declarations of war and peace

The Crown can declare war without the permission of Parliament.

Making treaties

The Crown has authority to make treaties with foreign countries.

The Issue of passports

The Crown controls the issue of passports

EXAMPLE: 'DOMESTIC' PREROGATIVES

Appointment of the Prime Minister

The monarch appoints the Prime Minister.

Dissolution of Parliament

The monarch retains the power to summon and to dissolve Parliament.

Royal assent

The monarch has the power to give royal assent to an Act of Parliament and must do so before it can come into force.

Who exercises the power?

It is also possible to make a distinction between powers which are exercised by the monarch personally and those which are exercised by the government in the name of the Crown. In this way, the Queen retains the power to appoint the Prime Minister and to prorogue and dissolve Parliament, whereas the government exercises prerogative powers such as the making of international treaties and the granting of passports.

FURTHER THINKING

The continuing existence of prerogative powers is the cause of some concern for those who would prefer to see all state power accountable to Parliament. There have been attempts to table legislation to bring such powers under the control of Parliament but the government inevitably fails to support such measures – preferring to retain the powers without interference from Parliament. One important example which can be used to enhance your answer has been the recent discussion surrounding the use of prerogative power by the government to agree an extradition treaty with the USA without the approval of Parliament. Many view the treaty as 'one-sided', giving far greater powers to the USA than to the UK. For discussion of the issues, see: Smith (2005); Harrington (2006).

Because prerogative powers are a residue of the original powers of the monarch, it is not possible to create new prerogative powers.

BBC v. *Johns* (Inspector of Taxes) [1965] Ch 32

Concerning: the possibility of creating new prerogative powers

Facts

The BBC attempted to argue that, because it had been established by Royal Charter, it was part of 'the Crown' and so exempt from paying tax.

Legal principle

It was held that the BBC could not escape paying taxes in this way. The historical exemption from taxation which applied to the Crown could not be extended to the Corporation. In a famous comment, Lord Diplock stated: 'it is 350 years and a civil war too late for the Queen's court to broaden the prerogative.'

However, there would seem to be a fine line between creating a new prerogative and merely re-interpreting an old one.

Malone v. *Metropolitan Police Commissioner (No. 2)* [1979] Ch 344

Concerning: the widening of prerogative

Facts

The plaintiff, an antiques dealer, was tried on charges of receiving stolen goods. During the trial it was revealed that his telephone had been tapped on the basis of a warrant issued by the Secretary of State. The plaintiff asserted that the Crown had no power, either under statute or common law, to tap telephones.

Legal principle

It was held that, because there was no express law against telephone tapping, the Secretary of State's actions were lawful. There was also an acknowledgement that, because there had existed a historical prerogative power to intercept letters, there must also be a power to intercept telephone calls.

Prerogative powers and statute

It is established that, where a prerogative power and a statutory power come into conflict, the statutory power will prevail. This is another expression of the doctrine of parliamentary sovereignty.

Attorney General v. De Keyser's Royal Hotel Ltd [1920] AC 508

Concerning: conflict between statutory and prerogative power

Facts

During the First World War, the hotel had been used by British troops. After the war, the owners sought compensation from the British government for damage caused to the building. A statutory power, under the Defence of the Realm Act 1914 provided for compensation payments but the government argued that their actions did not fall under the Act but, instead, fell under the prerogative power of defence and so no compensation was payable.

Legal principle

It was held that, where a statute is passed, it replaces the prerogative power.

EXAM TIP

Although *Attorney General v. De Keyser's Royal Hotel* established that a statutory power will take priority over a prerogative power, it seems that the prerogative power does not disappear completely but is 'kept in abeyance' while the statute is in force and can return if the statute is repealed. This is the kind of point which can greatly enhance your answers on this topic.

Prerogative powers and the courts

One of the most important aspects of prerogative powers is that, traditionally, they have not been enforceable by the courts. They have been seen as 'non-justiciable', which means that the court will recognise that a prerogative power applies in a given situation but cannot enforce it. This made such powers largely unaccountable.

Gouriet v. Union of Post Office Workers [1978] AC 435

Concerning: the courts and prerogative power

Facts

The union planned a strike in support of the anti-apartheid movement in South Africa. The Attorney General decided not to pursue legal action to prevent the strike. This led to accusations that he had misused his powers in order to protect the union.

KEY CASE

> **Legal principle**
> It was held that this was a prerogative power which was vested in the Attorney General. Consequently, it was not open to the court to question how, or whether, the power was used.

However, this position began to change with the recognition by the courts that prerogative powers were not beyond their jurisdiction.

KEY CASE

> *Council of Civil Service Unions* v. *Minister for the Civil Service (the 'GCHQ Case')* [1985] AC 374
>
> **Concerning: the courts and prerogative power**
>
> Facts
> It was decided by the government that workers at the secret Government Communications Headquarters (GCHQ) should not be allowed to join a trade union in case this led to them going on strike. The government altered, by means of prerogative power, the terms of employment of the workers to prohibit union membership. The union sought judicial review of the policy.
>
> Legal principle
> It was held that, although this particular prerogative power remained non-justiciable, there was nothing in principle to prevent the courts from considering the use of prerogative powers. This has led to various prerogative powers being challenged in later cases.

Problem area

The 'GCHQ case' is extremely important, even though the union lost their challenge to the policy. The key point is that the court recognised that it had the power to review some prerogative powers – this had previously been thought impossible.

Constitutional conventions

The other 'special source' is the constitutional convention. These are customs or historical practices which determine what will happen in certain circumstances. As with Royal Prerogative, conventions are not enforceable by the courts and so are described as 'non-legal' rules.

Problem Area

There is a considerable overlap between the operation of constitutional conventions and royal prerogative and this can cause confusion. The best way to view the relationship between the two is that certain actions are authorised by Prerogative power and the convention provides the custom or rule which dictates how the power shall be exercised.

EXAMPLE: CONSTITUTIONAL CONVENTIONS

Royal assent

The monarch gives Royal assent by means of prerogative power – the convention is that the monarch will always give assent to a Bill which has been approved by Parliament.

Appointment of the Prime Minister

The Monarch appoints the Prime Minister – by convention this is the leader of the political party with the largest number of seats in the House of Commons.

Vote of confidence

By convention, the government will resign if it loses a vote of confidence in the Commons.

There is nothing in law to enforce a convention and it is said that the sanction is 'political' rather than 'legal'. Conventions can also change over time.

FURTHER THINKING

The changing nature of conventions is particularly evident in relation to ministerial responsibility. The convention that Ministers would resign if there were serious failings in their department has all but disappeared and this can be viewed in terms of a weakening of the 'political' sanction. For a discussion of recent development of constitutional conventions see Wilson (2004).

Chapter Summary:
Putting it all together

☐ Can you tick all the points from the revision checklist at the beginning of this chapter?

☐ Take the **end-of-chapter quiz** on the companion website.

☐ Test your knowledge of the cases below with the **revision flashcards** on the website.

☐ Attempt the essay question from the beginning of the chapter using the guidelines below.

☐ Go to the companion website to try out other questions.

Answer guidelines

See the essay question at the start of the chapter.

Points to remember when answering this question
Use a clear introduction to make, briefly, the distinction between a written and an unwritten constitution. Emphasise the absence of a central document in the UK constitution and the overlapping nature of the various sources of constitutional law.

Address the various sources in turn, making the distinction between 'ordinary' and 'special' sources. Begin with statute and common law, which apply to this area in the same way as other areas of law. Therefore, you need to utilise examples to illustrate relevance.

In considering the 'special' sources, acknowledge the degree of overlap between prerogative powers and constitutional conventions. Use the examples above to demonstrate how such unwritten powers operate within the constitution.

Draw your answer together with a sizeable conclusion (not just a couple of lines) which reflects on the characteristics of the various sources. As statute and common law are well known, your answer should concentrate on prerogative powers and conventions.

Make your answer really stand out
Always use examples to support your arguments. Many students do not include cases, etc. and this is always penalised.

Indicate that you are aware of the impact of other aspects of the constitution on the question (such as the separation of powers and the doctrine of parliamentary sovereignty). You need not examine these in detail, but it will greatly enhance your answer to have acknowledged their relevance to the debate.

Emphasise the essentially uncertain nature of the UK constitution and, perhaps, draw some brief comparison with countries which have a written constitution. Even a modest attempt at comparison will impress the examiner, but do not digress too much – make the point and then move on.

FURTHER READING

Blackburn, R. (2004) 'Monarchy and the Personal Prerogatives', *Public Law* 546–63.

Cohn, M. (2005) 'Medieval Chains, Invisible Inks: On Non-Statutory Powers of the Executive', 25 *Oxford Journal of Legal Studies* 97.

Dicey, A.V. (1885) *An Introduction to the Study of the Constitution*, 10th edn (1959). London: Macmillan.

Harrington, J. (2006) 'Scrutiny and Approval: The Role for Westminster Style Parliaments in Treaty Making', 55 *International and Comparative Law Quarterly* 121.

Pontin, B., Billings, P. (2001) 'Prerogative Orders and the Human Rights Act: Elevating the Status of Orders in Council', *Public Law* 21–7.

Smith, R. (2005) 'Right and Wrongs: Going Over There', 102.24 *Law Society Gazette* 18.

Squires, D. B. (2000) 'Judicial Review of the Prerogative after the Human Rights Act', 116 *Law Quarterly Review* 572–5.

Wilson, Lord (2004) 'The Robustness of Conventions in a Time of Modernisation and Change', *Public Law* 407.

3

Basic principles of the constitution

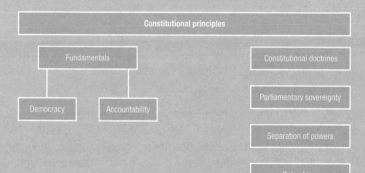

A printable version of this topic map is available from
www.pearsoned.co.uk/lawexpress

Revision Checklist

What you need to know:

- [ ] The constitutional importance of the principles of democracy and accountability.

- [ ] The three constitutional doctrines which underpin the operation of the constitution: parliamentary sovereignty; the separation of powers; and the rule of law.

- [ ] The separation of powers as a mechanism for preventing the over concentration of power and the danger that power will be abused as a consequence.

- [ ] The rule of law as a means of ensuring that all are treated fairly and that no-one is above the law.

- [ ] The traditional approach towards parliamentary sovereignty, which holds that Parliament is the most powerful organ of state, and the extent to which this principle has been undermined by our membership of the European Union.

Introduction

The constitution may be unwritten but it operates in accordance with a number of fundamental principles.

We saw in Chapter 2 that the unwritten constitution has a number of sources, but there are also broader principles which dictate how 'the system' operates. Some of these can be described as 'constitutional doctrines' and they provide fundamental rules which dictate how the constitution works. These doctrines are common examination topics and so need to be understood. They can also be discussed in answers on other aspects of the constitution.

Essay question advice

The constitutional doctrines are common essay topics. In answering questions, examiners will expect you not only to state what the doctrines are but also to provide some analysis, typically couched in terms of 'how important are the doctrines to the operation of the constitution' or 'to what extent have the doctrines changed'. This second type of question is particularly common in relation to parliamentary sovereignty, which has been dramatically undermined by our membership of the EU, and examiners will want to see some understanding of how this has changed the operation of parliamentary sovereignty.

Problem question advice

Problem questions on the rule of law and the separation of powers are relatively uncommon, as both lend themselves more readily to essay questions. However, examiners may choose to set a problem question on parliamentary sovereignty. As with essay questions, such problem questions will require you to outline the key aspects of parliamentary sovereignty and, crucially, to illustrate how this has been affected by EU membership.

Sample question

Could you answer this question? Below is a typical problem question that could arise on this topic. Guidelines on answering the question are included at the end of this chapter, whilst a sample essay question and guidance on tackling it can be found on the companion website.

Problem question

Warmsea is a South Coast seaside resort represented in Parliament by the fiercely patriotic Conservative, Rodney Smith.

At his constituency surgery, Rodney sees Charlie Roper, owner of Glamcabs, the luxury taxi company which relies heavily for its income on the executives who visit the seafront conference centres which are central to Warmsea's economy. Having recently invested over £200,000 in a new fleet of luxury cars Charlie is outraged to hear of an impending EU Regulation imposing a 900 cc maximum on engines in taxis as part of a policy of reducing emissions by public transport on environmental grounds. Faced with either selling his new fleet at a loss or paying for a costly engine conversion for each car, Charlie is determined to fight and is looking to his MP for support.

The following week, at Prime Minister's Questions, Rodney confronts the Prime Minister and asks him to ignore the Regulation. In response he is told that the UK, as a member state of the EU, is obliged to implement EU provisions whatever the reservations of individual MPs, although the position would have been slightly different had this been a Directive rather than a Regulation. Rodney is far from satisfied by this answer and accuses the Prime Minister of cowardice. 'This is the British Parliament and we are supreme', says Sir Rodney.

Is Sir Rodney correct in his view?

■ Basic principles of the constitution

In considering how the constitution operates, there are a number of general themes or principles which must be recognised as exerting an influence. These include the so-called 'constitutional doctrines' of the **separation of powers**, the **rule of law** and

parliamentary sovereignty, but there are also principles which are even more fundamental to how the state operates and these should also be considered.

Democracy

The UK is a democracy and the principle that those in power are in office because they have been elected is central to the operation of the state. The parliamentary process reflects the will of the people who have elected their MPs to represent them and to pass legislation in their name. Similarly, it is the fact that the House of Lords has traditionally not been elected which has presented the greatest pressure for change.

EXAM TIP

In describing the constitution, remember to emphasise that the shift from an all-powerful monarch to a democracy represents one of the most important influences on the constitution over the past 300 years. The fact that this process is still ongoing can be seen in the proposals for an elected House of Lords, replacing appointment by the Prime Minister with election by the people.

Accountability

Closely linked to the principle of democracy is the requirement for accountability within the constitution. Those in power must be accountable for the way in which they use their powers so that power cannot be abused. For example, civil servants are accountable to the minister who heads their department and the minister is accountable to Parliament. In this way, much of the operation of the constitution is concerned with making sure that the mechanisms for ensuring accountability work properly.

REVISION NOTE

Increasing accountability for the use of power is a theme which recurs throughout the study of constitutional and administrative law and can be seen in discussions on areas such as judicial review, parliamentary scrutiny and ministerial responsibility. When writing about the operation of the state, always demonstrate that you have considered this aspect of the debate and can show how those in power are held to account.

■The separation of powers

The doctrine of the separation of powers is a simple, but crucial, principle which underpins the way in which power is used by the state. Remember that, originally, all power was concentrated in the hands of the monarch and, consequently, it was almost impossible to prevent the abuse of such powers. For this reason, power within the modern constitution is divided between a number of key 'organs of state', which are considered in the next chapter. They oversee each other and have to work together to achieve their objectives. This serves either to prevent the abuse of power by any one part of the state or at least to limit its impact.

The doctrine recognises that the division of power between the various organs of state is not always amicable and there are often tensions as one part of the state seeks to exert control over another. This is particularly true of the relationship between the executive and the courts.

The 'soft' separation of powers

The contrast is sometimes made between countries such as the USA, which are seen as having a very rigid separation of powers between the organs of the state, and the UK, where there is often said to be a 'soft' separation. All this means is that there is a little more flexibility in the UK system, which allows the various elements of the state to work together.

Composition and powers

Power in the UK is divided between the three organs of state: the legislature, the executive and the judiciary. Read Chapters 5–7 for more detail on each of these. It must be recognised that the powers of the monarch are now mostly symbolic.

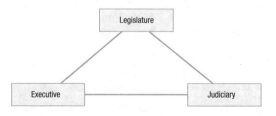

Overlapping personnel

It might be thought that a separation of powers requires different people to work within the three organs of state, but this is clearly not the case in the UK.

The Queen

Strictly speaking, the Queen is a member of all three organs of the state, with 'the Queen's government', 'the Queen in Parliament' and 'the Queen's judges'. However, within the modern constitution, the monarch is a largely symbolic presence, which does not impact on the overall division of power within the state.

Ministers

A more important overlap is that of ministers who are members of the Cabinet (the executive) and also members of Parliament (the legislature). Note that it is not essential that a member of the Cabinet also be an MP, but most are.

Law Lords

Judges who sit in the House of Lords (the highest court in the land) are also members of the House of Lords (the upper chamber of the legislature) however they do not participate in purely political debates as this would compromise their judicial independence.

Problem area The House of Lords

Students frequently become confused when discussing the House of Lords and do not make it clear whether they are referring to the House of Lords as a court or as a legislative chamber. Always be clear which you mean, as such confusion greatly undermines your answers.

The Lord Chancellor

One of the most important changes in recent years has been to the role of the Lord Chancellor. Formerly, the Lord Chancellor was a member of all three organs of state, being a member of the Cabinet, Speaker of the House of Lords and head of the judiciary, but his powers have been radically altered by the Constitutional Reform Act 2005.

The powers of the Lord Chancellor			
	Legislative function	Executive function	Judicial function
Pre-CRA 2005	Speaker of the House of Lords	Member of the Cabinet	Head of the judiciary
			Appoints judges
Post-CRA 2005	Replaced by 'Lord Speaker'	Member of the Cabinet	Replaced as Head of Judiciary by Lord Chief Justice
			Judicial appointments now made by Judicial Appointments Commission

Constitutional Reform Act 2005

The 2005 Act makes a number of important changes to the constitution, including the creation of a Supreme Court. In relation to the Lord Chancellor, the Act replaces him as head of the judiciary with the Lord Chief Justice and replaces him as Speaker of the House of Lords with the 'Lord Speaker'.

FURTHER THINKING

The changing role of the Lord Chancellor has been one of the most radical modifications to the constitution in recent years and has been the subject of heated debate. Many have argued that the Lord Chancellor fulfilled a vital role in communicating between the various organs of state, whereas others have suggested a political bias to the role. For a discussion of the key issues, see Woodhouse (2007).

The separation of powers in practice

The most important aspect of the separation of powers is the way in which the organs of state act to restrain each other and prevent the other institutions from exceeding their powers.

M v. *Home Office* [1994] 1 AC 377

Concerning: accountability of the executive to the courts

Facts

M arrived in the UK from Zaire, claiming political asylum, but his application was refused. The Home Secretary ordered his deportation but the High Court ordered the Home Secretary not to proceed with the deportation until the court had considered the case. The Home Secretary ignored the court order and M was deported.

Legal principle

The Home Secretary was held to be in contempt of court for refusing to comply with the order of the court. The fact that he was a minister of the Crown did not place him above the law and so the court could restrain him in the exercise of his powers.

KEY CASE

R v. *Secretary of State for the Home Department, ex parte Anderson* [2003] 1 AC 837

Concerning: power to set life sentences

Facts

A was convicted of two murders and received the mandatory life sentence. The trial judge recommended that he serve at least 15 years but the Home Secretary increased this to 20 years. The court had to consider whether the courts or the Home Secretary should set sentences for such prisoners.

Legal principle

It was for the courts and not the Home Secretary to set sentences. This was a judicial function and the involvement of a politician in the process contravened the right to a fair trial.

KEY CASE

R v. *Secretary of State for the Home Department, ex parte Fire Brigades Union* [1995] 2 AC 513

Concerning: power of the executive to ignore legislation

Facts

The Criminal Injuries Compensation Scheme operated under royal prerogative but was replaced by provisions of the Criminal Justice Act 1988, which allowed the Home Secretary to introduce a statutory scheme at a later date. Five years later, the Home Secretary had still not introduced the statutory compensation scheme and decided, instead, to amend the original scheme.

Legal principle

It was held that when an Act of Parliament allows a minister to decide when the provisions should come into force, this is not the same as allowing the minister to ignore the Act altogether. It is for Parliament to change the statute – not the minister.

EXAM TIP

In discussing the separation of powers, always emphasise the tensions which exist between the organs of state, particularly the judiciary and the executive. The separation of powers is not an amicable arrangement but rather a potential conflict, with each part of the state determined to retain their powers.

■The rule of law

The second constitutional doctrine is the rule of law, which can be a difficult principle to understand because there is not one simple 'rule' and there have been a number of different interpretations of the term. Basically, the rule of law is a set of underlying principles which governs how the legal system should operate and how the powers of the state should be controlled.

EXAM TIP

Exam answers on the rule of law are often weak and rambling. Impress the examiner by not only stating what the various definitions are but also by following this with some consideration of whether the various definitions appear to be reflected in our system. Even a relatively modest discussion will set your answer apart from the majority, which are simply descriptive.

Problem area Defining the Rule of Law

Students frequently struggle to define the rule of law in their answers and this can lead to confusion. Make reference to some of the following definitions to demonstrate your broader understanding of what the term is taken to mean.

Definitions of the rule of law

Writer	Key features
Joseph Raz (1979)	▮ Law should be general, open and clear. ▮ Law should be stable. ▮ Judiciary should be independent. ▮ Law should not be biased. ▮ Courts able to review state powers. ▮ Courts should be accessible.
'Declaration of Delhi' (1959)	▮ Representative government. ▮ No retrospective law. ▮ Respect for human rights. ▮ The right to challenge the state. ▮ Right to a fair trial.
Albert Dicey (1885)	▮ No arbitrary power. ▮ State power should be specified in law. ▮ No punishment except for breach of the law. ▮ Law applies to all persons equally.

Main principles

The most important common principle in the above definitions is that no-one should be above the law, including the state itself, and that the state should only be able to act in accordance with the law and not in an arbitrary way (i.e. as it sees fit).

KEY CASE

Entick v. *Carrington* (1765) 19 State Tr 1029

Concerning: the limits of state powers

Facts

The King's messengers broke into Entick's house on orders from the Secretary of State to seize both Entick and his papers (he was suspected of treason). Entick challenged the legality of the search but the Secretary of State argued that such powers were an essential part of government.

Legal principle

The state had to act within legal authority. Therefore, if there was no statute or common law precedent which authorised the search, it would be illegal. The state was not above the law.

■ Parliamentary sovereignty

Of all the constitutional doctrines, parliamentary sovereignty is the most fundamental principle guiding the operation of the state and it draws on the themes of democracy and accountability mentioned earlier. Put simply, the doctrine states that Parliament is the supreme body within the constitution.

EXAM TIP

Parliamentary sovereignty is a popular topic for examiners and it is possible to score high marks with a structured approach. Always remember to address the question in two parts: first, setting out how the doctrine applied (prior to EU membership) and then explaining how it has been undermined by membership of the EU. Also, remember to include as many examples as possible from statute and case law – this will make your answer really stand out!

Problem area Sovereignty and the separation of powers

There is a potential for confusion when considering parliamentary sovereignty and the separation of powers. The separation of powers seems to suggest that the organs of the state can oversee each other to prevent the abuse of power but parliamentary sovereignty allows Parliament to override any other part of the state. The simplest way to approach this is to remember that, ultimately, one body has to have control to prevent deadlock and that, in a democracy, that should be the elected body – Parliament.

Definition of sovereignty

The most commonly applied definition of parliamentary sovereignty comes from Dicey, who suggested three key rules:

1. Parliament can make or unmake any law

If there were areas of law which Parliament could not change then that would suggest that someone was telling Parliament what to do and, therefore, that Parliament was not sovereign.

His Majesty's Declaration of Abdication Act 1936

In 1936 King Edward VIII wished to marry American divorcee Wallis Simpson, causing a constitutional crisis, as it was widely believed that the country would not accept Simpson as their Queen. In order to marry, Edward gave up the throne but this required an Act of Parliament to take effect. In this way, the monarch could not act without the agreement of Parliament.

Union with Ireland Act 1800

This united England and Ireland. In this way, Parliament was able to alter the physical limits of the state and the land which it covered, bringing the people of Ireland under the sovereignty of Parliament.

Parliament Act 1911

In 1909 the House of Lords refused to pass the budget approved by the House of Commons. This was seen as the unelected Lords challenging the elected Commons and so Parliament introduced the 1911 Act to restrict the power of the Lords to delay legislation. In this way, Parliament was able to legislate over its own procedures and the way in which the law is made.

2. Parliament cannot bind its successors

Because it is the institution of Parliament which is sovereign, each successive Parliament can change the legislation passed by previous Parliaments. This means that the 2007 Parliament can change legislation made by the 2006 Parliament. Similarly, the 2007 Parliament cannot pass a statute which could not be changed by the 2008 Parliament. If this were not the case then there would be areas of law which Parliament could not affect, which would break Dicey's first rule.

KEY STATUTE

Ireland Act 1949

In 1800 Parliament passed the Union with Ireland Act, which stated that England and Ireland should, 'from the first day of January ... and for ever after, be united into one kingdom.' In 1949 Parliament granted Ireland its independence from England. The fact that the 1800 Parliament had intended a permanent union did not prevent Parliament from passing the later Act.

This raises the 'doctrine of implied repeal', which states that, if an Act of Parliament is inconsistent with an earlier statute, the later Act is taken to repeal the first.

KEY CASE

***Vauxhall Estate Ltd v. Liverpool Corporation* [1932] 1 KB 733**

Concerning: the doctrine of implied repeal

Facts

The corporation took the plaintiff's property under a compulsory purchase order. In calculating the compensation to be paid, the corporation wanted to rely on the terms of the Housing Act 1925, but the plaintiff argued that the calculation should be based on the (more generous) terms of the Acquisition of Land (Assessment of Compensation) Act 1919.

Legal principle

It was held that the provisions of the later Act should apply.

---

3. No-one can question Parliament's laws

Although the rule speaks of 'no-one', the key issue is whether the courts can challenge Parliament. Under the traditional model of parliamentary sovereignty, the answer is 'no'.

KEY CASE

British Railways Board v. *Pickin* [1974] AC 765

Concerning: the power of the court to challenge Parliament

Facts

P sought to challenge the British Railways Act 1968, arguing that the statute was invalid as there were irregularities in the procedure which had led to it being passed.

Legal principle

It was held that it was not for the court to examine how an Act of Parliament had come into force or to question the correctness of the procedures employed within Parliament. If the statute had been passed by Parliament, the role of the court was simply to apply the provisions.

Parliamentary sovereignty and EU law

Having established that Dicey's rules apply, we need to consider the impact of our membership of the EU on parliamentary sovereignty.

Problem area The EU and sovereignty

Membership of the EU has had a dramatic effect on parliamentary sovereignty, so you must include it in any answer. You also need to refer to the specific provisions and cases if you are to achieve a high mark.

KEY STATUTE

European Communities Act 1972, section 2

General implementation of Treaties

(1) All such rights, powers, liabilities, obligations and restrictions from time to time created or arising by or under the Treaties ... are without further enactment to be given legal effect or used in the United Kingdom shall be recognised and available in law, and be enforced, allowed and followed accordingly.

The reference to 'without further enactment' is crucial, as this means without Parliament.

EXAM TIP

In addition to mentioning section 2(1), also make reference to section 2(4), which states that the provisions apply to 'any enactment passed or to be passed', meaning that the 1972 Act bound Parliament to the EU law which existed at the time but also to EU law passed in the future. This is the sort of point which will gain you extra credit in the exam.

Regulations and Directives

EU provisions implemented in the form of Regulations or Directives also have implications for parliamentary sovereignty. In particular, because regulations are 'directly applicable', they do not require an Act of Parliament to come into force, thereby further undermining parliamentary sovereignty.

Type of provision	Features
Regulation	▌ General in application (applies to all member states). ▌ Binding in its entirety. ▌ Directly applicable (requires no Act of Parliament to take effect).
Directive	▌ Specific in application (applies only to certain member states). ▌ Binding as to the result to be achieved. ▌ Not directly applicable (requires an Act of Parliament to take effect).

KEY CASE

R v. *Secretary of State for Transport, ex parte Factortame Ltd (No. 2)* **[1991] 1 AC 603**

Concerning: the supremacy of EU over UK law

Facts

Spanish fishermen sought to avoid fishing quotas by registering their ships in the UK. The government introduced legislation to counter this, but the fishermen argued this was contrary to EU law.

Legal principle

It was held that, where there was conflict between EU and domestic law, the courts must give effect to the EU provisions. The law of Parliament could be set aside.

Francovich v. *Italy case c-9/90* [1991] ECRI-5357

Concerning: Non implementation of EU Directives

Facts

The Italian state failed to implement an EU Directive which ensured that employees of insolvent companies would be paid wages owed to them.

Legal principle

It was held that, as the Italian state had failed in its obligation to implement the Directive, it must compensate individuals who had suffered loss as a consequence.

Chapter Summary:
Putting it all together

TEST YOURSELF

- [ ] Can you tick all the points from the revision checklist at the beginning of this chapter?
- [ ] Take the **end-of-chapter quiz** on the companion website.
- [ ] Test your knowledge of the cases below with the **revision flashcards** on the website.
- [ ] Attempt the problem question from the beginning of the chapter using the guidelines below.
- [ ] Go to the companion website to try out other questions.

Answer guidelines

See the problem question at the start of the chapter.

Points to remember when answering this question
Remember that the examiner wants to see both description and analysis in your answer. This means that you should set out the relevant law clearly before moving on to offer some application. In this way, a good answer to this question will first explain how parliamentary sovereignty works and then illustrate how EU membership has eroded the doctrine.

Begin by setting out the principle of parliamentary sovereignty, making reference to

Dicey's three tests. Provide examples of each and show how they contribute to the overall proposition that Parliament is supreme within the constitution.

Then address the scenario, which requires you to consider EU Regulations and Directives. Explain the impact of the European Communities Act 1972 and the decision in *Factortame*, before highlighting the difference between Regulations and Directives (that Regulations are directly applicable and so become part of UK law without Parliament, whereas Directives require an Act of Parliament to take effect).

Conclude that there is little scope for the Prime Minister and the government to avoid their obligations under EU law and little scope for Parliament to challenge the provisions.

Make your answer really stand out

Mention that, even in the case of Directives, the UK government could be sued in the European Court for failing to implement the provisions of the Directive following the decision in *Francovich* v. *Italy* (1991).

Point out that, although the government is bound to follow EU law, which undermines parliamentary sovereignty, this is only because Parliament enacted the European Communities Act 1972. Under Dicey's tests, Parliament could repeal the Act at any time, thereby removing the UK from the EU and regaining sovereignty. For political and economic reasons this is very unlikely to happen, but it *is* possible, and the examiner will give you credit for recognising this point.

FURTHER READING

Barendt, E. (1995) 'Separation of Powers and Constitutional Government', *Public Law* 599–619.

Craig, P. P. (1997) 'Formal and Substantive Conceptions of the Rule of Law: An Analytical Framework', *Public Law* 467–87.

Dicey, A. V. (1885) *An Introduction to the Study of the Constitution*, 10th edn (1959). London: Macmillan.

Elliott, M. (1999) 'The Demise of Parliamentary Sovereignty? The Implications for Justifying Judicial Review', 115 *Law Quarterly Review* 119–37.

Elliott, M. (2004) 'Parliamentary Sovereignty Under Pressure', 2 *International Journal of Constitutional Law* 545.

Griffith, J. A. G. (2001) 'The Common Law and the Political Constitution', 117 *Law Quarterly Review* 42–67.

Jowell, J. (2006) 'Parliamentary Sovereignty Under the New Constitutional Hypothesis', *Public Law* 562–80.

Raz, J. (1979) *The Authority of Law: Essays on Law and Morality*. Oxford: OUP.

Williams, D. (2000) 'Bias, Judges and the Separation of Powers', *Public Law* 45–60.

Woodhouse, D. (2007) 'The Constitutional Reform Act 2005: Defending Judicial Independence the English Way', 5 *International Journal of Constitutional Law* 153.

4
Institutions of state 1

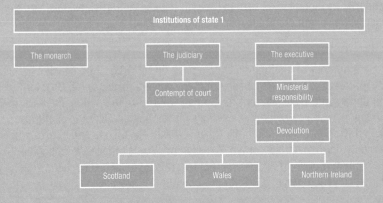

A printable version of this topic map is available from
www.pearsoned.co.uk/lawexpress

Revision Checklist

What you need to know:

- [ ] The constitutional position of the monarch as a head of state who retains largely symbolic powers in relation to the operation of the state
- [ ] The importance within the constitution of the independent judiciary which can act to protect the individual from abuse of state powers
- [ ] The function and forms of contempt of court as a means of ensuring the administration of justice
- [ ] The composition and function of the executive and the relationship betweeen the state and its ministers (including the process of devolution)
- [ ] The development of ministerial responsibility as a constituitonal convention

Introduction

The 'state' comprises a number of institutions which have to work together.

There are a number of institutions which make up the 'state' and which use the powers given to them under the separation of powers discussed in Chapter 3. You need to understand their different functions within the constitution and examiners will want to see that you can identify how they work together. Over the centuries, power has shifted from the monarch to the other institutions of state and students need to be clear on where power lies within 'the system'. You also need to understand the role of both contempt of court and ministerial responsibility as mechanisms which contribute (in very different ways) to the operation of the state.

Essay question advice

Possible essay questions might involve consideration of how ultimate power within the constitution has shifted from the monarch to the other institutions of state. You may also be asked to explore the operation of government and the relationship between Prime Minister, Minister and civil servants – possibly within the context of ministerial responsibility. In all cases, the examiner will be looking for both an understanding of the composition and function of the various state institutions, and an appreciation of the relative strengths and weaknesses of the system. Therefore, description must be accompanied by analysis and criticism.

Problem question advice

Both contempt of court and ministerial responsibility are common topics for exam questions and, in both cases, examiners will be looking for an appreciation of how the law has changed. Questions on contempt of court will usually centre on the impact of the Contempt of Court Act 1981 and questions on ministerial responsibility will be looking for discussion of the changing nature of this constitutional convention. As with other areas, the best answers will utilise examples to support their arguments.

Sample question

Could you answer this question? Below is a typical problem question that could arise on this topic. Guidelines on answering the question are included at the end of this chapter, whilst a sample essay question and guidance on tackling it can be found on the companion website.

Problem question

Roland Dutton is a senior civil servant in the Department of Transport, with responsibility for the introduction of a new computerised ticketing system for the London Underground. Determined to make a name for himself with this high profile project, he refuses all offers of assistance and delivers the project on time, largely by cutting corners during the testing programme. His minister, George Shaw, is kept informed in general terms but takes little real interest in the detailed progress of the project. Cobb, who is a colleague of Dutton, warns the minister that the testing programme appears superficial, but he is ignored. The introduction of the new system is a disaster, with the entire underground network gridlocked for a week. The cost to the economy is estimated in billions and seven people are trampled to death in the confusion of overcrowded tube stations.

The minister is called to the House to explain the fiasco and the Transport Select Committee call both Dutton and Cobb to explain their role in the development of the system. Prior to appearing before the Committee, Cobb is summoned by the minister and told that he should make no mention of his earlier warning when giving evidence.

There is growing pressure on George Shaw to resign over the issue, but the minister refuses stating that there is no precedent for him to resign over such a matter and that, in any event, this is merely an operational mistake for which he cannot and should not be held responsible.

Discuss.

The monarch

Although the UK is a parliamentary democracy, it retains a monarch as head of state. As such, the monarch presides over events such as the state opening of Parliament and acts as host to foreign heads of state when they visit the UK. What has changed over the past 300 years, however, is the extent of the real power exercised by the monarch within the constitution.

REVISION NOTE

Although you are highly unlikely to face an exam question solely on the monarch, it is a subject which features in many possible exam questions, as part of topics such as the royal prerogative, the separation of powers and parliamentary sovereignty. The diminishing powers of the monarch is one of the most important themes underpinning the development of the modern constitution, so examiners will give credit for mention of this as part of the discussion.

Centuries ago, all power within the state was in the hands of the monarch. Now, because of parliamentary sovereignty and the separation of powers, most of the power originally exercised by the monarch lies elsewhere. That is not to say, however, that the monarch is unimportant.

The monarch is currently:

- Head of state.
- Head of the Commonwealth.
- Head of the Church of England.
- Commander in Chief of the Armed Forces.

In addition, the monarch has the following powers:

- Summoning and dissolving Parliament.
- Appointing the Prime Minister.
- Appointing ministers.
- Declaring war.

The judiciary

The next key institution of state is the judiciary. Although the term covers all judges, it is those who sit in the higher courts (most obviously the House of Lords) who are most important to the operation of the constitution, as they are in a position to challenge the government and ensure that it functions within the law.

The independent judiciary

The constitution of the UK places great emphasis on the independence of the judiciary – i.e. that they are not influenced or controlled by the government of the day. Only if the judiciary is free from such control can it act in the best interests of the people when the government exceeds its powers. Factors which emphasise this independence include:

▌ Judges are immune from liability for the decisions they reach.
▌ By convention, ministers will not criticise judges or the decisions they reach in particular cases.
▌ Ministers and MPs will not comment on cases currently before the courts (also known as *sub judice*).
▌ Judges must not actively participate in politics.
▌ Senior judges (High Court, Court of Appeal and House of Lords) cannot be removed from office without a resolution passed by both Houses of Parliament.

EXAM TIP

Emphasise the importance of an independent judiciary and the way in which the government relies on this. Public inquires, such as those into the Hillsborough disaster, 'Bloody Sunday' or the Hatfield rail crash, are always chaired by a senior judge to emphasise the independence of the proceedings.

Contempt of court

The law prohibits actions which bring the administration of justice into disrepute. This falls under the heading of 'Contempt of Court', which can be either civil or criminal.

Civil contempt	▌ Refusal to obey an order of the court
Criminal contempt	▌ Scandalising the court (attacks on the impartiality or integrity of a judge) ▌ Contempt in the face of the court ▌ Publication prejudicial to the course of justice

R v. *New Statesman (Editor). ex parte DPP* (1928) 44 TLR 301

Concerning: scandalising the court

Facts

The New Statesman magazine published an article in which it was stated: 'an individual owning to such views ... cannot apparently hope for a fair hearing in a court presided over by Mr Justice Avory.'

Legal principle

It was held that this brought the integrity of the judge into disrepute and so constituted a contempt of court.

Morris v. *Crown Office* [1970] 2 QB 114

Concerning: contempt in the face of the court

Facts

A group of students disrupted a sitting of the High Court by singing and shouting slogans.

Legal principle

The judge instantly sentenced the ringleaders to three months' imprisonment. The power to do so was upheld on appeal.

Sunday Times v. *United Kingdom* (1979) 2 EHRR 245

Concerning: publications prejudicial to the course of justice

Facts

The Sunday Times was prevented by injunction from publishing an article on the Thalidomide drug scandal at a time when the parties to the case were engaged in negotiations to reach a settlement.

Legal principle

The case went to the European Court of Human Rights, where the UK law was found to breach Article 10 (right to freedom of expression). This led to the passage of the Contempt of Court Act 1981.

Contempt of Court Act 1981

Note that the law on publications by newspapers, etc. is now governed by the Contempt of Court Act 1981.

Contempt of Court Act 1981, section 2

Limitation of scope of strict liability

(1) The strict liability rule applies only in relation to publications, and for this purpose 'publication' includes any speech, writing, [programme included in a programme service] or other communication in whatever form, which is addressed to the public at large or any section of the public.
(2) The strict liability rule applies only to a publication which creates a substantial risk that the course of justice in the proceedings in question will be seriously impeded or prejudiced.
(3) The strict liability rule applies to a publication only if the proceedings in question are active within the meaning of this section at the time of the publication.

■The executive

An 'executive' is a body which formulates and implements policy. However, in the study of constitutional and administrative law, the term is generally used to mean the government. The way in which the executive operates and interacts with the other institutions of state is a crucial aspect of the study of the constitution.

The Prime Minister

The executive is led by the Prime Minister, who is responsible for the overall conduct of the government and for the appointment of the ministers who head each of the departments (transport, health, defence, etc.).

The Cabinet

The Cabinet is comprised of the ministers who head each of the departments (Secretaries of State) together with ministers responsible for government business in the Commons (Leader of the House) and the Lords (Lord Privy Seal).

Ministers

Each department has a minister who takes responsibility for the way in which the department functions and the extent to which it achieves its objectives.

Ministerial responsibility

Ministers are bound by two constitutional conventions which fall under the heading 'ministerial responsibility'.

Problem area Examples of ministerial responsibility

Because ministerial responsibility is a constitutional convention, it is a 'non-legal' rule and so not enforced by the courts. This means that examples are not decided cases but are simply 'political events'.

Collective ministerial responsibility

When a decision is reached by the Cabinet, all ministers must publicly support that decision, even if they opposed it during the Cabinet discussions. If a minister cannot do this, then they must resign from the government.

KEY CASE

The 'Westland Affair'

Concerning: collective ministerial responsibility

Facts

The UK's last military helicopter company was for sale. The Prime Minister, Margaret Thatcher, favoured a US buyer, but the Defence Secretary, Michael Heseltine, favoured a European bid. Heseltine was outvoted and resigned from the Cabinet, as he felt he could not publicly support the decision.

Legal principle

A minister who cannot stand by the decision of the Government in public cannot retain their post.

Individual ministerial responsibility

Each government department has many thousands of civil servants working within it. Such civil servants are not directly accountable to Parliament as it is the minister who must explain the operation of the department. In this way, if there is a serious error within the department, it is the minister who should assume 'individual ministerial responsibility' and, ultimately, resign.

The convention has changed dramatically over the years, so that now it is highly unusual for a minister to resign because of failings within their department.

KEY CASE

The 'Crichel Down Affair'

Concerning: individual ministerial responsibility

Facts

A plot of land which had been requisitioned by the army during the Second World War was transferred to the Ministry of Agriculture after the war. The original owners of part of the land wished to reclaim it but their claim was mishandled by the Ministry. As a result, the minister, Thomas Dugdale, resigned.

Legal principle

This is generally seen as the 'classic' example of individual ministerial responsibility. Dugdale was in charge of the department and so felt obliged to resign.

Examples of individual ministerial responsibility resignations after Crichel Down

Lord Carrington (1982)	Resigned over the invasion of the Falkland Islands (his staff failed to predict the invasion)
Leon Brittan (1986)	Resigned in the aftermath of the Westland affair (his staff leaked a letter from the Attorney General to the press)
Stephen Byers (2002)	Resigned after allegations of misleading Parliament over the failure of Railtrack, the company set up to manage the UK rail network

There are, however, many more ministers who have held on to their jobs, despite widespread calls for them to resign.

Examples of individual ministerial responsibility non-resignations

William Whitelaw (1982)	Faced calls for his resignation after an intruder reached the Queen's bedroom
James Prior (1984)	Faced calls for his resignation after mass escape from the Maze Prison in Belfast
Michael Howard (1995)	Faced calls for his resignation over mass prison escapes

49

Problem area Personal resignations

When considering the question of ministerial resignations, be careful not to include those following 'personal indiscretion' such as Cecil Parkinson, Tim Yeo, David Blunkett and Peter Mandleson. In these cases, ministers resigned because their personal conduct raised questions over their integrity, not because of errors within their departments. Therefore, they are not examples of ministerial responsibility.

Why do ministers lose their jobs?

Remember that a minister's chances of holding on to their job owe more to political circumstances than to the facts of the case. In this way factors which influence a minister's chances include:

▌ Is Parliament sitting? (A scandal during the summer break is less likely to result in a resignation as MPs are not in Parliament to create pressure on the minister.)
▌ Personal popularity with the Prime Minister.
▌ Popularity with the party.
▌ World events (the media are easily distracted by a disaster or other 'big story').

FURTHER THINKING

The changing nature of the convention of ministerial responsibility is a key area of change within the constitution and examiners will give credit for a broader understanding of the debate. By considering the reasons why ministers are far less likely to resign than in the past, it is possible to demonstrate precisely the analytical skills which examiners are looking for. Read Bamforth (2005) for an overview of the issues.

Devolution

Another key aspect of the executive is the shift under the current government towards devolution.

KEY DEFINITION

Devolution. The process by which power is given (or 'devolved') from Westminster to Scotland, Wales and Northern Ireland, giving them greater control over their own affairs and the power to make their own laws in certain areas. This is not full independence, however, as Westminster retains power over key areas such as defence.

Devolution	
Scotland	Scotland Act 1998 created Scottish Executive and Scottish Parliament. Does not have powers over areas such as defence, foreign affairs, immigration, finance and economic matters.
Wales	Government of Wales Act 1998 created Welsh Assembly, which has fewer powers than the Scottish Parliament.
Northern Ireland	Northern Ireland Assembly created by the 1998 'Belfast Agreement' (also known as the 'Good Friday Agreement'). The Assembly has been suspended a number of times but came back into power in May 2007.

Problem area Devolution

Although the process of devolution should be the same for Scotland, Wales and Northern Ireland, the result has been very different. Scotland has far more power over its own affairs than Wales and the process in Northern Ireland has been dogged by delay and argument between the political parties. In discussing the topic be careful not to treat all three cases as the same, because each country's experience of devolution has been different.

Chapter Summary:
Putting it all together

TEST YOURSELF

☐ Can you tick all the points from the revision checklist at the beginning of this chapter?

☐ Take the **end-of-chapter quiz** on the companion website.

☐ Test your knowledge of the cases below with the **revision flashcards** on the website.

☐ Attempt the problem question from the beginning of the chapter using the guidelines below.

☐ Go to the companion website to try out other questions.

Answer guidelines

See the problem question at the start of the chapter.

Points to remember when answering this question
Do not jump straight to individual ministerial responsibility – take some time to outline the nature of collective responsibility as well.

Point out that it is the minister and not the civil servant who is accountable to Parliament.

The central issue is the degree to which the minister should accept responsibility for the actions of Dutton. It might be argued that the minister was unaware of Dutton's activities (which would tend to undermine arguments for his resignation) but he was informed by Cobb and this would tend to undermine the minister's position.

The pressure placed on Cobb to lie to Parliament is extremely serious. Misleading Parliament has prompted resignations in the past.

Make your answer really stand out
Include examples from recent history. Remember, because ministerial responsibility is a convention, there are no decided cases but you should use examples to illustrate your points. All too often, students forget to use such examples and this greatly undermines their answers.

FURTHER READING

Bamforth, N. (2005) 'Political Accountability in Play: The Budd Inquiry and David Blunkett's Resignation', *Public Law* 229–38.

Brazier, R. (1994) 'It is a Constitutional Issue: Fitness for Ministerial Office in the 1990s', *Public Law* 431–51.

Hadfield, B. (2005) 'Devolution, Westminster and the English Question', *Public Law* 286–305.

Longley, D., Lewis, N. (1996) 'Ministerial Responsibility: The Next Steps', *Public Law* 490–507.

Reid, C. (2003) 'The Limits of Devolved Legislative Power: Subordinate Legislation in Scotland', 24 *Statute Law Review* 187.

Scott, R. (1996) 'Ministerial Accountability', *Public Law* 410–26.

Steyn, Lord (2006) 'Democracy, the Rule of Law and the Role of Judges', 3 *European Human Rights Law Review* 243–53.

Trench, A. (2006) 'The Government of Wales Act 2006: The Next Steps on Devolution for Wales', *Public Law* 687–96.

5
Institutions of state 2

A printable version of this topic map is available from
www.pearsoned.co.uk/lawexpress

Revision Checklist

What you need to know:

- [ ] The composition and structure of the legislature
- [ ] The legislative function of Parliament
- [ ] The passage of primary and secondary legislation and the relationship between the two forms of provision
- [ ] The scrutiny function of Parliament and the effectiveness of the various mechanisms for scrutiny
- [ ] The nature and scope of parliamentary privilege

Introduction

Of all the institutions of state, Parliament has the most important functions to perform.

The previous chapter considered the role of the monarch, judiciary and executive within the constitution. This chapter examines the work of the final institution of state: the legislature (Parliament). Remember, under the doctrine of parliamentary sovereignty outlined in Chapter 3, Parliament is the most powerful of the institutions of state. Therefore, you must be able to discuss the work of Parliament and consider its contribution to the operation of the state.

Essay question advice

Essay questions on the scrutiny function of Parliament are quite common. The important point to remember is that the examiner will not just want a list of the various mechanisms for scrutiny but will also want to see some assessment of their effectiveness. It is this analytical element to your answer which will gain the higher marks.

Problem question advice

Problem questions on Parliament usually centre on the operation of parliamentary privilege, and often require you to differentiate between the absolute privilege enjoyed by MPs and the qualified privilege enjoyed by the media. Here examiners will want to see a clear understanding of the differences between the two forms of privilege and also the ability to apply the rules to the facts of the scenario.

Sample question

Could you answer this question? Below is a typical essay question that could arise on this topic. Guidelines on answering the question are included at the end of this chapter, whilst a sample problem question and guidance on tackling it can be found on the companion website.

One of the key functions of Parliament is to scrutinise the operation of the executive. Assess how effective the existing parliamentary mechanisms for scrutiny are in achieving this objective.

REVISION NOTE

Remember that any consideration of the role of Parliament must acknowledge the doctrine of parliamentary sovereignty. Therefore, when discussing the functions of Parliament, it is important to emphasise that it is because Parliament is sovereign that it is Parliament (rather than any of the other institutions of state) which creates statute and scrutinises the work of the executive.

Problem area Parliament and executive

One of the most common mistakes made in exams is to confuse legislature and executive. Always be clear that the legislature is Parliament (comprising of over 600 MPs), whereas the executive is the government or Cabinet of ministers.

Also, it can be confusing to have to jump between the terms 'legislature' and 'Parliament', depending on the discussion. Discussions on the separation of powers speak of 'the legislature', whereas answers on parliamentary sovereignty, speak of 'Parliament'. Don't worry too much about which term you use as long as you do not confuse it with the executive.

■ The legislature

The UK has a 'bicameral legislature' (i.e. composed of two chambers). These are the House of Commons and the House of Lords.

The House of Commons

The House of Commons is the dominant chamber, as it is elected and so has a democratic mandate. The party with the most seats in the House of Commons forms the government.

Total Number of MPs	646
Labour	352
Conservative	196
Lib Dem	63
Others	35
Government majority at last election	64

FURTHER THINKING

Note that the above numbers are the result of the 'first past the post' election system, which is widely criticised for not being truly representative of votes cast. Successive governments have resisted introducing a system of proportional representation (PR), as it would reduce their majority and force them to work more closely with their opponents, but many argue that a proportional system would be fairer. For discussion of the issues, see the report of the Jenkins Commission (1998).

The House of Lords

The House of Lords is known as the 'second chamber' and is not elected, being largely appointed. It is often referred to as a 'revising chamber', there to advise the Commons and serve as a 'voice of reason'.

Total number of Lords	738
Labour	211
Conservative	205
Lib Dem	77
Crossbench	207
Bishops	26
Other	12

FURTHER THINKING

Reform of the House of Lords is a topical issue and examiners will give credit for an understanding of the difficulties faced by the government in trying to modernise the upper House, particularly as there seems to be little agreement on the best way forward. For an overview of the discussion, see Phillipson (2004).

■ Functions of Parliament

There are two key functions of Parliament: legislation and scrutiny.

Legislation

Parliament approves between 60 and 70 Bills per year, creating Acts of Parliament. There are various types of Bill:

Public Bill	Affects everyone
Private Bill	Applies to specific people or organisations
Private Member's Bill	Introduced by an MP who is not a member of the government

Legislative process

First reading	The title of the Bill is read out in the House of Commons
Second reading	The responsible minister sets out the purpose of the Bill to Parliament and the opposition responds. Then there is a debate in the House
Committee stage	The Bill is referred to a standing committee, which considers the Bill line by line and may make amendments
Report stage	The Bill is reported back to the House, which may accept or reject any amendments
Third reading	Largely a formality to correct any errors
The Lords	The Bill is sent to the Lords. The above process is repeated in the Lords
Royal assent	Announced in the Commons and the Lords

Parliament Act 1911, section 2(1)

If any Public Bill (other than a Money Bill or a Bill containing any provision to extend the maximum duration of Parliament beyond five years) is passed by the House of Commons [in two successive sessions] (whether of the same Parliament or not), and ... is rejected by the House of Lords in each of those sessions, that Bill shall, on its rejection [for the second time] by the House of Lords, unless the House of Commons direct to the contrary, be presented to His Majesty and become an Act of Parliament on the Royal Assent being signified thereto, notwithstanding that the House of Lords have not consented to the Bill.

Primary and secondary legislation

It is important to differentiate between primary and secondary legislation.

Primary legislation

Primary legislation consists of the Acts of Parliament, discussed above.

Secondary legislation

Sometimes, an Act of Parliament (known as the 'parent Act') will give the power to make rules/ regulations/ codes of practice to a minister, a local authority or other department. Such rules/ regulations/ codes of practice are 'secondary legislation' (also known as 'delegated legislation' or 'subordinate legislation') and are used to save parliamentary time. The crucial differences between primary and secondary legislation are:

▌ Primary legislation is debated by Parliament. Secondary legislation is not.
▌ Primary legislation cannot be challenged by the courts. The operation of secondary legislation can be challenged by means of judicial review.

REVISION NOTE

The distinction between primary and secondary legislation is particularly important in relation to judicial review and the power of the courts to challenge the use of powers granted under secondary legislation.

Police and Criminal Evidence Act 1984, section 66

The Secretary of State shall issue codes of practice in connection with –
(a) the exercise by police officers of statutory powers –
    (i)   to search a person without first arresting him; or
    (ii) to search a vehicle without making an arrest;
(b) the detention, treatment, questioning and identification of persons by police officers;
(c) searches of premises by police officers; and
(d) the seizure of property found by police officers on persons or premises.

Scrutiny

Parliament also scrutinises the work of the executive to ensure the government is functioning effectively and not abusing its powers. This is achieved by a number of mechanisms:

Mechanism	Format	Advantages	Disadvantages
Prime Minister's Questions	30 minutes questions once a week	Puts the PM on the spot before Parliament	Theatrical, often has little substance
Ministerial Questions	Each minister must answer questions once every 3–4 weeks	Ministers are held to account and must provide information	Dull and poorly attended
Debates	Varies depending on type of debate	Forces government to justify its actions	Often very short and limited in number
Select Committees	Each Ministry has a Committee to oversee its work. The Committee can demand papers and call witnesses	Thorough and ongoing scrutiny of the government	Only advisory – have no powers to impose sanctions

EXAM TIP

In considering Parliament's scrutiny of the executive, always emphasise that some mechanisms (such as Prime Minister's Questions) are largely ineffective as methods of holding the government to account compared with others (such as select committees).

Problem area Committees

Be careful not to confuse *select* committees with *standing* committees. Select committees examine the work of a particular government department. Standing committees consider Bills as they pass through Parliament during their 'committee stage'.

▮Parliamentary privilege

One important aspect of Parliament which frequently features in examinations relates to the privileges which Parliament enjoys. These can be categorised as 'collective' and 'individual' privileges.

Collective privilege

These are the privileges which attach to Parliament as an institution and relate to matters such as admissions, expulsions and disciplinary matters. It is important to remember that Parliament makes its own rules and procedures, in much the same way as a club or society.

KEY CASE

Bradlaugh v. *Gossett* (1884) 12 QBD 271

Concerning: admission to take up a seat in Parliament

Facts

B had been elected but was an atheist and so would not swear the parliamentary oath to God, so the House of Commons refused to allow him to take his seat.

Legal principle

The court held that the jurisdiction of the House of Commons over its members was absolute – there was nothing the court could do.

Privilege and contempt

Any breach of privilege (i.e. breach of the rules of Parliament) amounts to contempt which can lead to Parliament imposing a punishment on MPs. Contempt of Parliament includes:

▮ Disorderly conduct.
▮ Misleading the House.
▮ Bribery and corruption.
▮ Refusing to co-operate with a Parliamentary Committee.

Punishments

Censure	MP receives a reprimand from the Speaker
Suspension	An MP can be suspended for contempt for a period from one day to the entire parliamentary session
Imprisonment	MPs can be imprisoned in Big Ben, outsiders taken to a prison (not used since 1880)
Expulsion	As the most serious punishment an MP can be expelled from the House

Individual privilege

As well as the collective privileges which attach to Parliament as an institution, there are also privileges which are enjoyed by MPs as individuals.

Freedom from arrest

MPs have freedom from arrest but this only applies to civil arrest, not an arrest relating to criminal offences. Therefore, this only really applies to arrest for contempt of court (e.g. non-payment of damages in a civil case) and so is not a meaningful protection for MPs.

EXAM TIP

When discussing freedom from arrest, make sure to point out that the immunity from arrest applies from 40 days before the parliamentary session begins to 40 days after the session ends. It is also worth noting that the privilege had far greater importance in the days of the debtor's prisons, when a person could be imprisoned for non-payment of a debt.

Freedom of speech

Of far greater significance is the freedom of speech which is enjoyed by MPs. This means that an MP is immune from suit for defamation (libel or slander) for anything said as part of 'proceedings in Parliament'. This is justified on the grounds that it allows Parliament to function more efficiently by permitting MPs to speak freely, without fear of legal action.

Dillon v. *Balfour* (1887) 20 LR Ir 600

Concerning: parliamentary privilege and freedom of speech

Facts

A minister made a statement in Parliament that a midwife had deliberately refused to attend to a pregnant woman. The midwife attempted to sue for slander.

Legal principle

The court refused to hear the action as the statement was covered by parliamentary privilege.

'Proceedings in Parliament'

The privilege enjoyed by MPs is absolute (i.e. it does not matter if the statement was deliberate and malicious) but applies only to 'proceedings in Parliament'. This clearly applies to speeches within Parliament, during debates, etc., but the position is less clear with communications which move outside the buildings themselves (e.g. letters).

Rivlin v. *Bilainkin* [1953] 1 QB 485

Concerning: the meaning of 'proceedings in Parliament'

Facts

The claimant in an action for defamation had obtained an injunction preventing the defendant from repeating the 'defamatory' statement. The defendant repeated the statement in a letter and delivered copies to a number of MPs. The letters were posted within the House of Commons in the House of Commons post office.

Legal principle

It was held that, as the allegations were purely personal in nature and did not concern the business of the House, they could not be 'proceedings in Parliament' and, therefore, were not covered by privilege.

KEY CASE

The 'Strauss Case' HC 227 (1957–58), HC Deb, vol 591, col 208 (8 July)

Concerning: the meaning of 'proceedings in Parliament'

Facts

George Strauss MP wrote to a minister complaining about the activities of the London Electricity Board. The minister passed the letter to the Board, who threatened to sue Strauss for libel.

Legal principle

The House of Commons Committee for Privileges held that this fell within 'proceedings in Parliament' and was, therefore, privileged, but a vote within the House of Commons rejected this and held that it was not 'proceedings in Parliament' and so did not attract privilege.

It seems, therefore, that 'proceedings in Parliament' is limited to statements and communications directly concerned with the business of Parliament, either conducted within the Chamber or, in the case of letters, etc., directly related to ongoing parliamentary business.

Reporting of statements made in Parliament

Although MPs enjoy absolute privilege in relation to statements made in Parliament, the position is different when those statements are reported by others. Here, the privilege may be absolute or qualified, depending on who reports the statement.

KEY STATUTE

Parliamentary Papers Act 1840

The Act confers absolute privilege on papers either produced by the House (e.g. *Hansard*) or authorised by the House.

Statements by third parties

The position is different again for newspapers and other publications which publish what has been said in Parliament. They cannot claim absolute privilege and can only claim the common law defence of qualified privilege, which requires the statement to be fair, accurate and without malice.

There is also a defence of qualified privilege under the Defamation Act 1996.

KEY STATUTE

> **Defamation Act 1996, section 15(1) and Schedule 1, paragraph 1**
>
> The publication of any report or other statement mentioned in Schedule 1 to this Act is privileged unless the publication is shown to be made with malice.
>
> A fair and accurate report of proceedings in public of a legislature anywhere in the world.

Chapter Summary:
Putting it all together

TEST YOURSELF

- [ ] Can you tick all the points from the revision checklist at the beginning of this chapter?
- [ ] Take the **end-of-chapter quiz** on the companion website.
- [ ] Test your knowledge of the cases below with the **revision flashcards** on the website.
- [ ] Attempt the essay question from the beginning of the chapter using the guidelines below.
- [ ] Go to the companion website to try out other questions.

Answer guidelines

See the essay question at the start of the chapter.

Points to remember when answering this question
The question does not just require you to list the mechanisms for scrutiny but also to assess their effectiveness.

Explain the requirement for the executive to be accountable to Parliament as the elected representatives of the people.

List the various mechanisms for scrutiny (see the diagram in this chapter, above) and offer some analysis as to their effectiveness.

Always remember to offer some conclusion as to how well the system of scrutiny operates (e.g. pointing out the effectiveness of mechanisms such as select committees compared to others such as Prime Minister's Questions).

Make your answer really stand out

Remember to relate the concept of parliamentary scrutiny to the doctrine of parliamentary sovereignty. Explain why it is inevitable that it should be Parliament, rather than any other institution of state, which scrutinises the work of the executive.

Rather than merely listing the mechanisms, give some brief explanation of how they operate.

In relation to Prime Minister's Questions, emphasise that the event is as much for party morale (to see the leader perform well in Parliament) as for real scrutiny.

FURTHER READING

Feldman, D. (2004) 'The Impact of Human Rights on the UK Legislative Process', 25 *Statute Law Review* 91.

Hazell, R. (2006) 'Time for a New Convention: Parliamentary Scrutiny of Constitutional Bills 1997-2005', *Public Law* 247–98.

Lester, A. (2002) 'Parliamentary Scrutiny of Legislation Under the Human Rights Act 1998', 4 *European Human Rights Law Review* 432–51.

McHarg, A. (2006) 'What is Delegated Legislation?', *Public Law* 539–61.

Oliver, D. (2006) 'Improving the Scrutiny of Bills: The Case for Standards and Checklists', *Public Law* 219–46.

Phillipson, G. (2004) ' "The Greatest Quango of them All", "A Rival Chamber" or "Hybrid Nonsense": Solving the Second Chamber Paradox" ', *Public Law* 352–79.

Report of the Independent Commission on the Voting System (Jenkins Commission Report) (1998). London: HMSO. Available online at http://www.archive.official-documents.co.uk/document/CM40/4090/4090.htm.

Squires, D. (2000) 'Challenging Subordinate Legislation Under the Human Rights Act', 2 *European Human Rights Law Review* 116–30.

6
Civil liberties and human rights

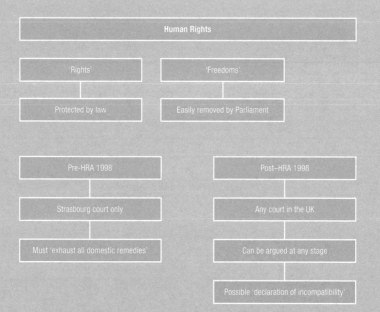

A printable version of this topic map is available from
www.pearsoned.co.uk/lawexpress

Revision Checklist

What you need to know:

☐ The traditionally precarious status of civil liberties in the UK as 'freedoms' rather than 'rights'

☐ The impact of the European Convention on Human Rights and how cases were brought before the European Court of Human Rights from the UK

☐ The impact of the Human Rights Act 1998

☐ The constitutional implications of the 1998 Act and the relationship between Parliament and the courts

☐ Current protections for human rights in the UK

■ Introduction

Increased protection for human rights is the most important development in UK law for generations.

The passage of the Human Rights Act 1998 was a huge step for the legal system and the constitution. Consequently, examiners will almost certainly make some reference to the Act in exams, either as a 'stand alone' topic or as part of a question on another subject. So the ability to discuss the Act and its implications will always help you to gain a higher mark.

Essay question advice

Essay questions on human rights in the UK and, in particular, the implications of the Human Rights Act 1998 are very common. Such questions require you to chart the development of human rights protection and it is possible to score highly, provided you are clear on the main stages in the process and remember to include plenty of examples.

Problem question advice

Problem questions are less common, but you may face a scenario based around an individual who wishes to enforce their rights before the courts. Here it is essential to have some knowledge of the individual Convention rights, together with an understanding of the procedure under the Human Rights Act 1998.

Sample question

Could you answer this question? Below is a typical essay question that could arise on this topic. Guidelines on answering the question are included at the end of this chapter, whilst a sample problem question and guidance on tackling it can be found on the companion website.

Essay question

Assess the impact of the Human Rights Act 1998 on the protection of individual rights in the UK.

■ Human rights in the UK

KEY DEFINITION

Rights. There is no single definition of the term 'rights', but a number of legal theorists have suggested possible meanings of the word. One of the most commonly cited definitions comes from Wesley Hohfeld who divided rights into 'privileges', 'claims', 'powers' and 'immunities'. The sorts of civil liberties which we normally think of when discussing rights would fall into Hohfeld's definition of a 'claim' right – we have a claim against the state to uphold our 'rights'.

There are three stages involved in considering the development of human rights protection in the UK: the traditional 'freedoms' model, the position under the European Convention on Human Rights and, finally, the current position following implementation of the Human Rights Act 1998. Any exam question on human rights in the UK will require you to describe these stages.

■ The traditional 'freedoms' model

If we think of a 'right' as something which we are able to do and which the state cannot take away, then the unwritten constitution of the UK has traditionally provided little protection for such rights.

REVISION NOTE

The topic of rights should be revised alongside Chapter 1 on the nature of the constitution and also the section in Chapter 3 on parliamentary sovereignty, since both topics play an important part in an understanding of the traditional approach to rights in the UK.

Remember that one of the key differences between the unwritten constitution of the UK and the written constitutions of most other countries is that the written constitution contains a number of fundamental rights (such as the right to bear arms in the USA). Also, the written constitution is a 'higher' source of law, which cannot be easily changed by the government. This means that such rights cannot ordinarily be taken away by the government.

In the UK the position has been very different. Here, there is no written constitution to form a 'higher' source of law and the doctrine of parliamentary sovereignty provides that there is no area where Parliament cannot legislate. This has meant that any so-called 'right' could be taken away by an Act of Parliament.

KEY STATUTE

Firearms (Amendment) Act 1997

Prior to the Dunblane School massacre in 1996, members of gun clubs had been allowed to keep properly registered guns. In the aftermath of the shooting, the government banned most handguns, thereby removing what gun owners saw as their 'right' to own guns.

KEY STATUTE

Hunting Act 2004, section 1

A person commits an offence if he hunts a wild mammal with a dog, unless his hunting is exempt.

The 2004 Act removed what hunters assumed to be their 'right' to hunt.

In this way, rather than having 'rights', citizens in the UK have enjoyed the 'freedom' to do anything which the state has not defined as illegal – which is not the same thing!

Problem area 'Rights' vs 'freedoms'

The distinction between 'rights' and 'freedoms' has been an important one. Examiners will credit an understanding of the distinction between the two and the different legal implications of each. In this way, be sure to emphasise the difference between a 'right', which can be claimed, and a 'freedom', which exists only until the state removes it.

■The European Convention on Human Rights

Signed in 1950, in response to the injustices of the Second World War, the Convention contains a number of fundamental human rights which are contained in its Articles:

Article 1 – Obligation on Signatories to respect human rights
Article 2 – the Right to Life
Article 3 – the Prohibition on Torture
Article 4 – the Prohibition on Slavery
Article 5 – the Right to Liberty and Security
Article 6 – the Right to a Fair Trial
Article 7 – the Right not to be Punished Except for Breach of the Law
Article 8 – the Right to Respect for Private Life
Article 9 – the Right to Freedom of Conscience, Thought and Religion
Article 10 – the Right to Freedom of Expression
Article 11 – the Right to Freedom of Assembly and Association
Article 12 – the Right to Marry
Article 13 – the Right to an Effective Remedy
Article 14 – the Prohibition on Discrimination (in relation to the Convention Rights)

Cases alleging breaches of Convention rights are heard by the European Court of Human Rights in Strasbourg.

EXAM TIP

When discussing human rights cases, always be careful not to become confused with EU law in general. For example, human rights cases are heard by the European Court of Human Rights (ECtHR) not by the European Court of Justice (ECJ).

■The European Convention and the UK

The European Convention was not incorporated into UK law until the passage of the Human Rights Act 1998. However, that is not to say that the Convention did not affect the law and the people of the UK. As signatories to the Convention, the UK government was bound to its terms as a matter of international law but, crucially, this did not confer rights on individual citizens.

Problem area The Convention and the UK

Understanding the relationship between the Convention and UK law before the 1998 Act came into force can be confusing. The principal point to remember is that, in order to uphold their Convention rights, UK citizens had to take a case to the Strasbourg Court and they could not do this until they had 'exhausted all domestic remedies' – i.e. been through the entire UK legal system, up to and including the House of Lords.

Where the UK was found to have breached Convention rights, the government usually changed the law to remove the inconsistency. This can be seen in the following example.

KEY CASE

Malone v. *Metropolitan Police Commissioner (No. 2)* [1979] Ch 344

Concerning: alleged breach of Article 8 (Right to Respect for Private Life)

Facts

The plaintiff argued that his telephone had been bugged by the police without lawful authority, thereby breaching his right to privacy.

Legal principle

The court refused to recognise that such a right existed in English law and held that no such right could be imported from Article 8 of the Convention.

KEY CASE

Malone v. *United Kingdom* (1984) 7 EHRR 14

Concerning: alleged breach of Article 8 (Right to Respect for Private Life)

Facts

Malone took his case to the European Court of Human Rights and argued the fact as above.

Legal principle

The ECtHR held that the telephone tapping powers in the UK did contravene Article 8, as they were not subject to clear and accountable legal procedures.

As a result, the UK Parliament passed the Interception of Communications Act 1985 to provide statutory authority for telephone tapping.

KEY STATUTE

Interception of Communications Act 1985, section 1(1), (2)

1 Subject to the following provisions of this section, a person who intentionally intercepts a communication in the course of its transmission by post or by means of a public telecommunication system shall be guilty of an offence and liable

   (a) on summary conviction, to a fine not exceeding the statutory maximum;

   (b) on conviction on indictment, to imprisonment for a term not exceeding two years or to a fine or to both.

2 A person shall not be guilty of an offence under this section if –

   (a) the communication is intercepted in obedience to a warrant issued by the Secretary of State under section 2 below; or

   (b) that person has reasonable grounds for believing that the person to whom, or the person by whom, the communication is sent has consented to the interception.

■ The Human Rights Act 1998

The 1998 Act made the Convention rights directly enforceable in the domestic courts. This means that, instead of having to go to the Strasbourg Court, a person can argue breaches of their rights under the Convention in any court in the UK. However, one important limitation is that the Convention rights are only 'vertically directly effective' (i.e. they can only be enforced against the state and not 'horizontally directly effective' (enforceable against other individuals). The Act defines this in terms of 'public authorities'.

KEY STATUTE

Human Rights Act 1998, section 6(1)

It is unlawful for a public authority to act in a way which is incompatible with a Convention right.

The role of the courts

One of the most important aspects of the Human Rights Act 1998 is the role of the courts in upholding the Convention rights. This has two key elements: first, as has already been noted, the 1998 Act allows claimants to argue breach of their Convention rights in the domestic courts, so judges in any court in the UK may be faced with issues of human rights which were previously reserved for the Strasbourg Court; secondly, when faced with such a claim, the courts must decide whether the UK law is consistent with or breaches the Convention right. This is a significant development of the court's role.

KEY STATUTE

Human Rights Act 1998, section 3(1)

So far as it is possible to do so, primary legislation and subordinate legislation must be read and given effect in a way which is compatible with the Convention rights.

Under section 3, the court must interpret the UK statute in a way which is compatible with the Convention rights if it is possible to do so.

FURTHER THINKING

The requirement imposed on the courts by section 3 is a marked departure from the traditional rules of statutory interpretation and sees the court potentially ignoring what Parliament intended in order to reconcile the domestic statute with the Convention right. For further discussion, see Kavanagh (2006).

Declarations of incompatibility

Although section 3 requires the court to interpret statutes in a way which is compatible with the Convention, there may be situations where the wording of the statute is so clear and unambiguous that it cannot be interpreted in any way other than in conflict with a Convention right. In such cases the court must make a 'declaration of incompatibility' (i.e. that the domestic statute is incompatible with the Convention).

KEY CASE

R (on the application of H) v. *London North and East Region Mental Health Review Tribunal* [2001] QB 1

Concerning: compatibility of domestic law with European Convention on Human Rights

Facts

H was detained in a mental hospital under the Mental Health Act 1983. He applied to the tribunal to be released but this required him to prove to the tribunal that the conditions for detention no longer applied. When his application was refused, H sought judicial review of the decision.

Legal principle

It was held that the requirement on H to prove that detention was no longer required imposed on him a reverse burden of proof which was incompatible with Article 5. Therefore, a declaration of incompatibility would be made.

KEY CASES

Wilson v. *First County Trust Ltd* [2002] QB 74

Concerning: compatibility of domestic law with European Convention on Human Rights

Facts

A loan agreement between the claimant and defendant pawnbrokers failed to correctly state the amount of credit. Section 127(3) of the Consumer Credit Act 1974 barred the court from enforcing the agreement.

Legal principle

The court held that the absolute bar on enforcement was an infringement of the right to a fair trial and the right to protection of property guaranteed by Article 6(1) of the European Convention.

If the court makes a declaration of incompatibility, it is open to Parliament to change the statute in order to remove the conflict with the Convention rights. Note that Parliament can also refuse to remedy the incompatibility, but there will be considerable political pressure on it to do so.

Remember that the final decision as to whether to alter the statute in question lies with Parliament – thereby retaining parliamentary sovereignty. The government had to include this in the Human Rights Bill in order for Parliament to approve it. Examiners will give you credit for recognising that Parliament still retains the ultimate power in such circumstances.

Chapter Summary:
Putting it all together

☐ Can you tick all the points from the revision checklist at the beginning of this chapter?

☐ Take the **end-of-chapter quiz** on the companion website.

☐ Test your knowledge of the cases below with the **revision flashcards** on the website.

☐ Attempt the essay question from the beginning of the chapter using the guidelines below.

☐ Go to the companion website to try out other questions.

Answer guidelines

See the essay question at the start of the chapter.

Points to remember when answering this question
Remember to address the three stages to the discussion: the original status of civil liberties in the UK as 'freedoms' rather than 'rights'; the process for enforcing Convention rights before the Human Rights Act 1998; and the position under the 1998 Act.

Spend some time considering the distinction between 'rights' and 'freedoms' and the examples (such as the post-Dunblane handgun legislation) which show how easily so-called 'rights' can be removed.

Do not forget to emphasise the problems with the system before the Human Rights Act 1998, most notably the requirement to 'exhaust all domestic remedies' before being allowed to pursue a case in the Strasbourg Court.

Emphasise the greater role for the courts following the Human Rights Act 1998 and, in particular, the ability of the court to make a 'declaration of incompatibility'.

Always produce a conclusion which addresses the question. In this case that requires some assessment of whether the position of the individual citizen has been improved by the 1998 Act. On the basis that we can now enforce Convention rights in the UK courts, the answer is probably 'yes'.

Make your answer really stand out

Highlight the fact that successive governments in the UK had refused to incorporate the Convention into UK law before 1998, fearing a 'flood' of cases, which has not in fact materialised.

Emphasise the increased role of the courts under the Human Rights Act 1998 and the difference between the duty under section 3 of the Act and traditional statutory interpretation.

Note that this increased role for the courts does not threaten parliamentary sovereignty because Parliament can still refuse to amend legislation following a declaration of incompatibility.

FURTHER READING

Arnull, A. (2003) 'From Charter to Constitution and Beyond: Fundamental Rights in the New European Union', *Public Law* 774–93.

Hickman, T. R. (2005) 'Constitutional Dialogue, Constitutional Theories and the Human Rights Act 1998', *Public Law* 306–35.

Hohfeld, W. (1919) *Fundamental Legal Conceptions: As Applied in Judicial Reasoning.* New Haven: Yale University Press.

Kavanagh A. (2006) 'The Role of Parliamentary Intention in Adjudication under the Human Rights Act 1988' 26 *Oxford Journal of Legal Studies* 179.

Klug, F. and Starmer, K. (2005) 'Standing Back from the Human Rights Act: How Effective Is It Five Years On?', *Public Law* 716–28.

Klug, F. and Wildbore, H. (2007) 'Breaking New Ground: the Joint Committee on Human Rights and the Role of Parliament in Human Rights Compliance', 3 *European Human Rights Law Review* 231–50.

Nicol, D. (2006) 'Law and Politics After the Human Rights Act', *Public Law* 722–51.

Steyn, Lord (2005) 2000–2005: Laying the Foundations of Human Rights Law in the United Kingdom', 4 *European Human Rights Law Review* 349–62.

7
Freedom of expression and assembly

Freedom of expression

Article 10 ECHR	Restrictions

Obscenity

Blasphemy

Official secrets

Racial hatred

Terrorism

Freedom of association

Article 11 ECHR	Restrictions

Assemblies	Processions

A printable version of this topic map is available from
www.pearsoned.co.uk/lawexpress

Revision Checklist

What you need to know:

- [ ] Some of the major restrictions on the right to freedom of expression in the UK
- [ ] The nature of public protest and the distinction between assemblies and processions
- [ ] The powers of the police in relation to the supervision and control of public assemblies
- [ ] The powers of the police in relation to the supervision and control of public processions

Introduction

We may have a right to freedom of expression but that does not mean that we can say what we like when we like.

Freedom of expression and freedom of assembly are seen as two of the most fundamental civil liberties, allowing us to speak freely and to protest publicly. However, these rights are not absolute and there are a number of restrictions on what we can say and how we can protest on the streets. Such restrictions illustrate the conflict between the civil liberties of the individual and the powers of the state. For this reason the topic is always popular with examiners.

Essay question advice

Essay questions on freedom of expression will usually ask you to provide an overview of the restrictions placed on free speech in the UK. Less common are questions which ask you to concentrate on one specific area, such as blasphemy or issues of race and religion. In all cases, remember not just to list the provisions but to also include some analysis of the supposed justification for state restrictions on free speech.

Problem question advice

Problem questions on freedom of association are always popular and usually require you to apply public order legislation to a scenario. Here the key is to be methodical and work through the relevant provisions, demonstrating how they relate to the facts of the question.

Sample question

Could you answer this question? Below is a typical problem question that could arise on this topic. Guidelines on answering the question are included at the end of this chapter, whilst a sample essay question and guidance on tackling it can be found on the companion website.

Problem question

Fircombe is an inner city estate which achieved notoriety last year following a weekend of racially motivated rioting and, although everyone has worked hard to establish some sense of community, there is still tension on the estate. Four houses in Jubilee Street are owned by Joshua Fiddler, a slum landlord, who has recently let them to families who have been evicted from local authority accommodation due to anti-social behaviour. Their children have quickly established themselves, with a spate of burglaries and car thefts and relations in the street are strained.

On Monday 21 June two of the youths steal a car and drive to the neighbouring Newcombe estate, which is predominantly Asian. During a police pursuit they lose control of the car, which mounts the pavement, seriously injuring a local man. The youths are arrested and when they are brought before the magistrates the following day bail is refused. Their families are furious and there is a disturbance in the court. Later that day the police receive reports that witnesses to the car crash have been threatened.

On the morning of Wednesday 23 June the local man dies in hospital and, at the local police station, Supt. Ellis receives a telephone call from Newcombe's community leaders, Anil and Sunil, who inform him that, because of the man's death, they have decided to bring forward July's annual Asian Pride march and hold it on Saturday 26 June instead. They provide Supt. Ellis with a proposed route for the procession which, as in previous years, will circle their estate. This takes the march along Warwick Street, which marks the boundary between the Newcombe and Fircombe estates. However, unknown to Supt. Ellis, Anil and Sunil plan to change the route on the day to take the march down Jubilee Street.

On Wednesday evening, Supt. Ellis learns that one of the youths has committed suicide in prison.

Advise Anil and Sunil on their obligations under public order legislation.

Advise Supt. Ellis of the steps he can take to diffuse the situation.

■ Freedom of expression

Freedom of expression (or freedom of speech) is seen as one of the most important of our civil liberties. It is safeguarded by Article 10 of the European Convention on Human Rights.

Problem area Freedom of expression and Article 10

Students frequently make the mistake of thinking that Article 10 guarantees free speech but this is not the case. Look at the wording of Article10 below and you will see that the state is still able to restrict free speech under certain circumstances.

KEY STATUTE

European Convention on Human Rights, Article 10

'Everyone has the right to freedom of expression. This right shall include freedom to hold opinions and to receive and impart information and ideas without interference by public authority.'

However, Article 10 continues to state that this right:

'... may be subject to such formalities, conditions, restrictions or penalties as are prescribed by law and are necessary in a democratic society.'

This means that the state can restrict free speech, providing that this is done in accordance with either statute or common law. There are a number of such restrictions, including the laws of obscenity, blasphemy, official secrets and more recent provisions relating to terrorism.

REVISION NOTE

When revising freedom of expression, remember to include the section on contempt of court in Chapter 4, as this is another important restriction on freedom of speech.

Obscenity

KEY STATUTE

Obscene Publications Act 1959, sections 1(1), 2(1)

'For the purposes of this Act an article shall be deemed to be obscene if its effect ... is, if taken as a whole, such as to tend to deprave and corrupt ...'

'... any person who, whether for gain or not, publishes an obscene article [or who has an obscene article for publication for gain (whether gain to himself or gain to another)] shall be liable.'

DPP v. *Whyte* [1972] AC 849

Concerning: meaning of 'tend to deprave and corrupt'

Facts

A husband and wife ran a bookshop which was raided by police who seized a large amount of pornography. It was argued that the customers of the shop could not be 'depraved and corrupted' by the pornography because they were used to such material.

Legal principle

It was held that '. . . the Act is not merely concerned with the once and for all corruption of the wholly innocent; it equally protects the less innocent from further corruption'.

Calder (John) (Publications) Ltd v. *Powell* [1965] 1 QB 509

Concerning: meaning of 'tend to deprave and corrupt'

Facts

A book was published depicting the life of a drug addict and highlighting the favourable aspects of drug taking.

Legal principle

It was held that obscenity was not confined to sexual matters. A book encouraging drug abuse could equally be termed 'obscene'.

Note the related, but little used, common law offences of 'conspiracy to corrupt public morals' and 'conspiracy to outrage public decency'.

Shaw v. *DPP* [1962] AC 220

Concerning: conspiracy to corrupt public morals

Facts

The defendant published a magazine containing contact details for prostitutes.

Legal principle

The House of Lords held that a conviction was justified in order 'to conserve not only the safety and order but also the moral welfare of the state'.

R v. *Gibson* [1990] 2 QB 619

Concerning: conspiracy to outrage public decency

Facts

The defendant staged an art exhibition containing a work made from a model head wearing two earrings, each made from a frozen three-month-old human foetus.

Legal principle

Regardless of whether there was a 'tendency to deprave and corrupt', an offence was committed where a public exhibition outraged public decency.

Blasphemy

Another restriction on freedom of expression is the common law offence of blasphemy, roughly defined as statements which are insulting or abusive to Christian belief. Although there are few modern prosecutions for blasphemy, it remains a possible charge.

R v. *Lemon* [1979] AC 617

Concerning: intention and blasphemy

Facts

The magazine Gay News published a poem depicting the life of Jesus and describing sexual acts committed on his body after crucifixion.

Legal principle

There was no requirement for an intention to blaspheme. All that was needed was the publication of material which was later held to be blasphemous.

R v. *Chief Metropolitan Stipendary Magistrate, ex parte Choudhury* [1991] 1 QB 429

Concerning: blasphemy and other religions

Facts

The claimant alleged that the novel *The Satanic Verses* by the author Salman Rushdie was blasphemous against Islam.

▶

Legal principle

The court held that the offence of blasphemy could only be committed against Christianity and did not extend to any other religion.

Official secrets

There are also offences arising from the disclosure of official secrets. This is now covered by the Official Secrets Act 1989, which creates a range of offences.

Offences under the Official Secrets Act 1989	
A member (or former member) of the security or intelligence services	'... if without lawful authority he **discloses any information**, document or other article relating to security or intelligence which is or has been in his possession by virtue of his position as a member of any of those services.' (section 1(1))
A person who is or has been a Crown servant or government contractor	'... if without lawful authority he **makes a damaging disclosure** of any information, document or other article relating to security or intelligence which is or has been in his possession by virtue of his position.' (section 1(3))
	'... if without lawful authority he **makes a damaging disclosure** of any information, document or other article relating to defence which is or has been in his possession by virtue of his position.' (section 2(1))
	'... if without lawful authority he **makes a damaging disclosure** of any information, document or other article relating to international relations ... which is or has been in his possession by virtue of his position' (section 3(1))
	'... if without lawful authority he **discloses any information** ... which is or has been in his possession by virtue of his position ... which – (i) results in the commission of an offence; (ii) facilitates an escape from legal custody; (iii) impedes the prevention or detection of offences.' (section 4)

Secretary of State for Defence v. *Guardian Newspapers Ltd* [1985] AC 339

Concerning: disclosure of official secrets

Facts

Sarah Tisdall, who worked in the Foreign Office, revealed to the Guardian newspaper the secret arrival of American nuclear missiles at a UK airforce base. Tisdall claimed that revealing this information was in the public interest.

Legal principle

It was held that she had contravened the Official Secrets Act and she was sentenced to six months' imprisonment.

R v. *Ponting* [1985] Crim LR 318

Concerning: disclosure of official secrets

Facts

Clive Ponting, an official within the Ministry of Defence, sent documents to an MP confirming that the government had misled Parliament over the sinking of the ship the General Belgrano during the Falklands War, with the death of 368 sailors. He was subsequently prosecuted under the Official Secrets Act.

Legal principle

The case was clearly proven and the judge directed the jury to convict but, instead, they acquitted Ponting, believing his claim that the disclosure was in the public interest.

Problem area Official Secrets Act 1911 and Official Secrets Act 1989

When discussing these cases, be sure to point out that both Tisdall and Ponting were charged under the Official Secrets Act 1911, which was later amended by the Official Secrets Act 1989.

FURTHER THINKING

The current provisions on official secrets continue to cause concern, with the fear that the state will use the law to prevent not only the disclosure of secrets, but also information which is simply embarrassing to the government and any examination answer should emphasise such concern. For a discussion of some of the cases in this area, see Bindham (2007).

Incitement to racial hatred

Further restrictions of freedom of expression have been introduced to combat racial and religious abuse.

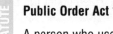

> **Public Order Act 1986, sections 18(1), 19(1)**
>
> A person who uses threatening, abusive or insulting words or behaviour, or displays any written material which is threatening, abusive or insulting, is guilty of an offence if –
>
> (a) he intends thereby to stir up racial hatred, or
> (b) having regard to all the circumstances racial hatred is likely to be stirred up thereby.
>
> A person who publishes or distributes written material which is threatening, abusive or insulting is guilty of an offence if –
>
> (a) he intends thereby to stir up racial hatred, or
> (b) having regard to all the circumstances racial hatred is likely to be stirred up thereby.

Similar provisions in relation to religious hatred are introduced by the Racial and Religious Hatred Act 2006, although these provisions are not yet in force.

Terrorism legislation

Restrictions on freedom of expression are also contained within the recent terrorism legislation.

> **Terrorism Act 2000, section 12(3)**
>
> A person commits an offence if he addresses a meeting and the purpose of his address is to encourage support for a proscribed organisation or to further its activities.

◼Freedom of association

Closely related to freedom of speech is the freedom of association – the freedom to protest in groups. This protest takes two forms: assemblies and processions.

As with freedom of expression, the freedom of association is protected under the European Convention but with similar limitations.

KEY STATUTE

European Convention on Human Rights, Article 11

'Everyone has the right to freedom of peaceful assembly and to freedom of association with others …'

However, Article 11 continues:

'… this article shall not prevent the imposition of lawful restrictions on the exercise of these rights by members of the armed forces, of the police or of the administration of the State.'

Assemblies

An assembly is defined as 'an assembly of 2 or more persons in a public place which is wholly or partly open to the air' (Public Order Act 1986, section 16). The Act allows the police to impose conditions on assemblies where certain conditions are satisfied.

KEY STATUTE

Public Order Act 1986, section 14(1)

If the senior police officer, having regard to the time or place at which and the circumstances in which any public assembly is being held or is intended to be held, reasonably believes that—

(a) it may result in serious public disorder, serious damage to property or serious disruption to the life of the community, or
(b) the purpose of the persons organising it is the intimidation of others with a view to compelling them not to do an act they have a right to do, or to do an act they have a right not to do,

he may give directions imposing on the persons organising or taking part in the assembly such conditions as to the place at which the assembly may be (or continue to be) held, its maximum duration, or the maximum number of persons who may constitute it, as appear to him necessary to prevent such disorder, damage, disruption or intimidation.

In this way, if the police believe that there will be serious public disorder, serious damage to property, etc., conditions can be imposed on the assembly.

Although this is the most commonly used power to control assemblies, you can also mention the ban on protests in the vicinity of Parliament under section 132 of the Serious Organised Crime and Police Act 2005 and the control on assemblies which trespass on land under section 14A of the Public Order Act 1986.

Processions

KEY CASE

***Flockhart* v. *Robinson* [1950] 2 KB 498**

Concerning: definition of a 'procession'

Facts

The defendant was accused of organising a political procession. This required the court to define what was meant in law by the term 'procession'.

Legal principle

It was held that a procession was 'not a mere body of persons: it is a body, of persons moving along a route'.

The situation in relation to processions is more complex but the basic principle is the same as for assemblies. If the police are satisfied that there is a risk of certain consequences, conditions can be imposed and (in extreme cases) the procession can be banned. With processions the question of notice must also be considered. In this way, there are three stages to considering a question on processions:

1 Has proper notice been given by the organisers to the police?
2 Are there grounds for imposing conditions on the procession?
3 What conditions could be imposed to remove the risk of disorder?

Problem area Processions

Many students trip up in examinations when answering questions on processions by immediately suggesting the imposition of conditions. Remember, the right to freedom of association should only be limited where absolutely necessary. Therefore, begin any answer from the position that the procession should be allowed to proceed unchanged, unless this will result in disorder. If this is not possible then the aim is to impose the *minimum* conditions necessary to remove the threat to public order.

Has proper notice been given by the organisers to the police?

Before we can answer this question we need to know whether the procession in question is one which is covered by the 1986 Act.

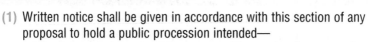

KEY STATUTE

Public Order Act 1986, section 11

(1) Written notice shall be given in accordance with this section of any proposal to hold a public procession intended—
  (a) to demonstrate support for or opposition to the views or actions of any person or body of persons,
  (b) to publicise a cause or campaign, or
  (c) to mark or commemorate an event,

  unless it is not reasonably practicable to give any advance notice of the procession.

(2) Subsection (1) does not apply where the procession is one commonly or customarily held in the police area (or areas) in which it is proposed to be held or is a funeral procession organised by a funeral director acting in the normal course of his business.

(3) The notice must specify the date when it is intended to hold the procession, the time when it is intended to start it, its proposed route, and the name and address of the person (or of one of the persons) proposing to organise it.

Therefore, the notice requirements can be summarised as follows, depending on the purpose of the procession:

Notice required	Notice not required
▮ Support or opposition for the views or actions of a person or persons	▮ Commonly or customarily held procession
▮ Publicise cause or campaign	▮ Funerals
▮ Mark or commemorate an event	

EXAM TIP

There is clearly a potential overlap between a procession to mark or commemorate an event (which requires notice) and a customarily held procession (which does not) and examiners will credit any recognition of this dilemma. Point out that the solution is to consider the other grounds as well to see if these are satisfied (e.g. publicise a cause or campaign).

Notice

The notice must specify:

- Date and time of procession.
- Route.
- Names of organisers.

The notice must be delivered to the police six days before the procession. Failure to provide notice is an offence. Note that the notice requirement applies only where this is 'reasonably practicable', so consider whether it is possible for the organisers to give notice (e.g. if the procession is a spontaneous reaction to events).

It is also an offence to deviate from the details contained in the notice (time, route, etc.) unless this is beyond the control of the organisers.

Are there grounds for imposing conditions on the procession?

Once notice has been received, the police assess whether the procession can proceed as planned. This is done by reference to section 12 of the 1986 Act.

Public Order Act 1986, section 12(1)

If the senior police officer, having regard to the time or place at which and the circumstances in which any public procession is being held or is intended to be held and to its route or proposed route, reasonably believes that—

(a) it may result in serious public disorder, serious damage to property or serious disruption to the life of the community, or
(b) the purpose of the persons organising it is the intimidation of others with a view to compelling them not to do an act they have a right to do, or to do an act they have a right not to do,

he may give directions imposing on the persons organising or taking part in the procession such conditions as appear to him necessary to prevent such disorder, damage, disruption or intimidation, including conditions as to the route of the procession or prohibiting it from entering any public place specified in the directions.

Conditions might include:

- Changing the date/time of the procession.
- Changing the route to avoid potential confrontation.

Banning processions

If the powers under section 12 are thought insufficient to prevent disorder, the police can apply to ban all processions in the area for a maximum of three months.

> **KEY STATUTE**
>
> **Public Order Act 1986, section 13(1)**
>
> If at any time the chief officer of police reasonably believes that ... the powers under section 12 will not be sufficient to prevent ... serious public disorder, he shall apply to the council of the district for an order prohibiting for such period not exceeding 3 months ... the holding of all public processions (or of any class of public procession so specified) in the district or part concerned.

Note that any ban affects *all* processions in the area, not just the one which formed the basis of the application/notice. This prevents the original organisation from simply changing its name in order to avoid the ban.

EXAM TIP

Although you should mention the possibility of a ban in any answer, it should be emphasised as the last resort for the police. Remember, the objective is to balance freedom of speech and public order – banning the procession (and freedom of speech) is a drastic measure not to be taken lightly, so make sure the examiner appreciates that you understand this point.

Chapter Summary:
Putting it all together

TEST YOURSELF

- [ ] Can you tick all the points from the revision checklist at the beginning of this chapter?
- [ ] Take the **end-of-chapter quiz** on the companion website.
- [ ] Test your knowledge of the cases below with the **revision flashcards** on the website.
- [ ] Attempt the problem question from the beginning of the chapter using the guidelines below.
- [ ] Go to the companion website to try out other questions.

Answer guidelines

See the problem question at the start of the chapter.

Points to remember when answering this question
You need to adopt a methodical approach to such questions, dealing with the following points in turn:

▌ Is this a 'procession' for the purposes of the 1986 Act? Almost all processions are covered but you need to show that you have established this point.
▌ Has adequate notice been served to the police? This should be done unless not 'reasonably practicable'.
▌ Do the circumstances suggest that conditions will be required?
▌ What are the minimum conditions required to remove the threat to public order?
▌ As a last resort, is a ban needed?

Make your answer really stand out
Show that you can balance the competing requirements of legitimate protest and public order. In this scenario, changing the routes of the procession might prevent disorder, but a procession which does not go anywhere near those with different views is unlikely to influence anything. Emphasise that you understand the dilemma this poses.

Show that you have worked through the questions in turn – do not jump in with 'the procession could be banned'.

Do not just state that conditions could be imposed – suggest what they might be (e.g. change of date/ time, change of route, etc.).

FURTHER READING

Bindham, J. (2007) 'Blowing the Right Whistle', 157 *New Law Journal* 602.
Hamilton, M. (2007) 'Freedom of Assembly, Consequential Harms and the Rule of Law: Liberty-Limiting Principles in the Context of Transition', 27 *Oxford Journal of Legal Studies* 75.
Jaconelli, J. (2007) 'Defences to Speech Crimes', 1 *European Human Rights Law Review* 27–46.
James, J. and Ghandi, S. (1998) 'The English Law of Blasphemy and the European Convention on Human Rights', 4 *European Human Rights Law Review* 430–51.
Kearns, P. (2000) 'Obscene and Blasphemous Libel: Misunderstanding Art'. *Criminal Law Review* 652–60.
Loveland, I. (2001) 'Freedom of Political Expression: Who Needs the Human Rights Act?', *Public Law* 233–44.
Sherlock, A. (1995) 'Freedom of Expression: How Far Should It Go?', 20(3) *European Law Review* 329–37.

8
Police powers

A printable version of this topic map is available from
www.pearsoned.co.uk/lawexpress

Revision Checklist

What you need to know:

☐ The constitutional status of police powers

☐ The importance and main scope of the Police and Criminal Evidence Act 1984 and Codes of Practice

☐ Powers of arrest available to police officers and the public

☐ Powers of stop search and search of premises available to police officers

☐ Legal requirements relating to police detention and questioning

Introduction

Police powers are the most visible example of the power of the state being used against the individual.

In Chapter 6 we considered the balance between the interests of the state and the civil liberties of the individual. Police powers represent one of the most important and most commonly used areas of state power. The police are one of the few elements of the state which is authorised to use force against the general public and so it is essential that police powers are clearly defined and controlled. The constitutional importance of police powers makes the topic a favourite with examiners.

Essay question advice

Essay questions on police powers can focus on a number of areas. Questions may ask you to consider whether the police have too much power or, alternatively, whether additional powers are needed. Questions might also ask you to assess the effectiveness of PACE 1984 in regulating police powers and preventing the abuse of power by officers. Such essays require both a knowledge of the provisions but also a critical approach to the purpose and function of police powers.

Problem question advice

Problem questions on police powers are much more common and can focus on any of the key areas, such as stop search, arrest, search of premises and the detention and questioning of suspects. Often questions will require you to consider a chain of events from initial contact, stop search and arrest, through to detention and questioning. In all cases, a clear knowledge of the relevant sections of PACE is essential, together with a methodical approach to applying the provisions.

Sample question

Could you answer this question? Below is a typical problem question that could arise on this topic. Guidelines on answering the question are included at the end of this chapter, whilst a sample essay question and guidance on tackling it can be found on the companion website.

Problem question

Barbara is a pensioner who returned home some weeks ago to find a burglar in her house. The man ran off but Barbara was able to give the police a detailed description of a pale, thin man in his early 20s, with short cropped fair hair. The man swore at her as he left and, consequently, she has also been able to tell the police that he had a Scottish accent. As there has been a spate of such burglaries in the area, the police have ensured that officers patrolling the area are aware of the description.

At 11.30 p.m. police constables Bradshaw and Smith see Kenny, a local youth with previous convictions for indecent exposure and assault, entering the street where Barbara lives. He is carrying a holdall. The officers recognise him instantly due to his long black hair and, when stopped and questioned, he tells them that he has been to the pub and is on his way to stay with a friend who lives nearby.

PC Bradshaw tells him that he is suspected of burglary and asks him to turn out his pockets but Kenny refuses. At this PC Smith snatches the holdall from Kenny and PC Bradshaw marches him into a nearby empty bus shelter, where he is ordered to remove his coat, shirt and shoes while Smith blocks the doorway. Although the search of Kenny's clothing reveals nothing, Bradshaw finds a screwdriver and a pair of gloves in the holdall. Kenny explains that his friend asked him to bring the screwdriver as he wanted to borrow it to fix his washing machine.

Kenny is taken to his friend's house which is empty and the police conduct a search after forcing an entry to the premises. In one of the bedrooms they find a small quantity of amphetamines and Kenny is arrested.

Assess the legality of the actions of the officers in this case.

■Police powers

Police powers are simply a way for the law to authorise conduct which would otherwise be illegal. For example, holding someone against their will would normally be false imprisonment but lawful arrest provides authority for detaining the person.

The Police and Criminal Evidence Act 1984 (PACE)

Any student hoping to answer examination questions on police powers must be familiar with the main provisions of the Police and Criminal Evidence Act 1984

(PACE). The Act governs all aspects of police contact with a suspect, from conducting stop search in the street to detention and questioning at the police station. The Act also has a small number of provisions which affect the presentation (and exclusion) of police evidence in court. Some of the key areas covered by PACE include:

Sections	Regulating
s. 1–5	Stop search of persons and vehicles
s. 8–23 and s. 32	Search of premises
s. 24–31	Powers of arrest
s. 34–65	Detention and questioning of suspects
s. 76	Confession evidence
s. 78	Exclusion of evidence at court

Codes of Practice

In addition to the provisions of PACE itself, there are also the Codes of Practice which contain the detailed rules governing key areas of police powers. These are divided into Codes of Practice A to H.

Code of Practice	Regulating
A	Stop search powers
B	Search of premises
C	Detention and questioning
D	Identification procedures
E	Tape recording of interviews
F	Visual recording of interviews
G	Powers of arrest
H	Detention and questioning in terrorism cases

EXAM TIP

Although examination answers will focus on the provisions of PACE, do not forget to mention the Codes of Practice and emphasise their importance. Examiners will give credit for an appreciation of the relationship between the statutory provisions and the Codes of Practice.

Background to PACE

The 1984 Act was introduced in response to widespread concern over the abuse of police powers in the early 1980s which culminated in a series of riots. The subsequent Scarman Report made a number of recommendations regarding police powers, many of which were incorporated into PACE 1984.

FURTHER THINKING

Although it is unlikely that you would face a question on the background to PACE, examiners will be impressed by any indication that you understand why PACE came into being and the tensions which underpin police powers. See the Scarman Report (1982).

Rice v. *Connolly* [1966] 2 QB 414

Concerning: the obligation to assist the police

Facts

A man was found by the police in an area where burglaries had occurred. When questioned, he refused to explain his presence or give his name and address. He was subsequently arrested for obstructing the police.

Legal principle

It was held that, although every citizen had a moral or social duty to assist the police, there was no relevant legal duty to that effect. Therefore, he had been entitled to decline to answer the questions put to him and (prior to his arrest) to accompany the police officer on request.

Stop search

The power to stop someone in the street and search them against their will has always been one of the most contentious police powers because, historically, people from ethnic minorities have been statistically more likely to be stop searched by the police. This led to calls for greater control over these powers.

Stop search is authorised by section 1 of PACE, which applies to the search of people and of vehicles. However, this only permits the police to search where there is a reasonable suspicion that certain, specified, objects will be found.

Students frequently make the mistake in examinations of not recognising that a search is only lawful when it is based on the reasonable suspicion that prohibited items will be found. In this way, the police cannot search to generate the reasonable suspicion – they must have the reasonable suspicion first.

What items justify a stop search?

Under section 1 of PACE, a search is authorised if the officer has reasonable suspicion that the person or vehicle is carrying one of the following prohibited items:

▮ Stolen items.
▮ Offensive weapons.
▮ Items intended for use in the commission of burglary, theft, deception, criminal damage or taking a vehicle without consent.
▮ Fireworks.

What constitutes 'reasonable suspicion'?

This can be difficult to establish but is important – if the officer does not have reasonable suspicion then the search may be unlawful.

KEY STATUTE

PACE, Code of Practice A

A person's race, age, appearance, or the fact that the person is known to have a previous conviction, cannot be used alone or in combination with each other as the reason for searching that person. Reasonable suspicion cannot be based on generalisations or stereotypical images of certain groups or categories of people as more likely to be involved in criminal activity. A person's religion cannot be considered as reasonable grounds for suspicion and should never be considered as a reason to stop or stop and search an individual.

Reasonable suspicion can sometimes exist without specific information or intelligence and on the basis of some level of generalisation stemming from the behaviour of a person. For example, if an officer encounters someone on the street at night who is obviously trying to hide something, the officer may (depending on the other surrounding circumstances) base such suspicion on the fact that this kind of behaviour is often linked to stolen or prohibited articles being carried.

Potentially Sufficient	Not sufficient
▌ Matches description	▌ Race
▌ Intelligence linking person to offences	▌ Religion
▌ Behaviour	▌ Appearance
	▌ Previous convictions

Problem area Previous convictions

It is very common for students to state that previous convictions justify a stop search – this is not so. Under PACE, the fact that a person has previous convictions for theft is not enough for the police to search them to see whether they are carrying stolen property.

EXAM TIP

Point out that, although drugs are not included in the above list, this does not mean that the police have no power to search a person for drugs – just that searches for drugs are authorised by the Misuse of Drugs Act 1971. The PACE powers are the most commonly used but there are also search powers under the Terrorism Act 2000 and the Criminal Justice and Public Order Act 1994. Mention these as an aside to your answer.

Where can a person be searched?

The powers under section 1 of PACE are 'street powers' (i.e. designed to be used on the street, not in the police station) and can only be exercised in a place where the public have access, by right or by permission (whether for payment or not). The powers do not apply in private dwellings. They also do not apply in the gardens of private dwellings, unless the officer has reasonable grounds to believe that the person to be searched is not the occupier of the house and is not there with the occupier's permission.

What can be searched?

As a 'street power', the search under section 1 is superficial and does not involve removing clothing. Therefore, an officer can only order a person to remove outer clothing, such as an outer coat, jacket or gloves.

What information must be given?

Before conducting the search, the officer must give the person being searched the following information:

 The officer's police station and name.
 The object of the search (i.e. what the officer believes the person is carrying).
 The grounds for the search (i.e why this person is being searched and not someone else).

After the search, the person is entitled to ask for a written record of the search (whether anything is found or not). They can ask for this within 12 months of the search.

Powers of arrest

The power of arrest is one of the most important police powers because it deprives a person of their liberty. Unlike stop search powers, which are only available to police officers, there are also powers of arrest available to the public: so-called 'citizen's arrest'. Therefore, in answering any question on arrest, you must first establish whether the person making the arrest is a police officer or not. This determines which powers should be applied. (Note that we are discussing arrest *without* warrant.)

You should view powers of arrest as a two-tier system: there are general powers of arrest which are available to everyone (PACE, section 24A) and an additional set of powers which are available *only* to police officers (PACE, section 24).

Powers of arrest available to members of the public

Whereas a police officer can make an arrest in relation to any offence, a member of the public can make an arrest only in relation to an indictable offence. Also, a member of the public cannot make an arrest in the belief that an offence is going to be committed – their powers of arrest only apply where:

 an offence *is being* committed (where a member of the public can arrest someone committing the offence or whom they have reasonable grounds to believe is committing the offence); or

▌ an offence *has been* committed (where a member of the public can arrest someone who has committed the offence or whom they have reasonable grounds to believe has committed the offence).

Note that the powers of arrest available to the general public apply only where an offence is committed – if no offence has been committed then there is no power of arrest.

Furthermore, the arrest is only authorised where two further conditions are satisfied:

KEY STATUTE

PACE, section 24A(3), (4)

(3) But the power of arrest is exercisable only if—
   (a) the person making the arrest has reasonable grounds for believing that for any of the reasons mentioned in subsection (4) it is necessary to arrest the person in question; and
   (b) it appears to the person making the arrest that it is not reasonably practicable for a constable to make it instead.
(4) The reasons are to prevent the person in question—
   (a) causing physical injury to himself or any other person;
   (b) suffering physical injury;
   (c) causing loss of or damage to property; or
   (d) making off before a constable can assume responsibility for him.

Powers of arrest available to police officers

The additional powers of arrest available to police officers are as follows:

▌ In relation to *all* offences (not just indictable offences).
▌ Anyone *about to* commit an offence (or anyone whom they have reasonable grounds to suspect is about to commit an offence).
▌ Whereas the powers of arrest available to the general public only apply where an offence is committed, a police officer can arrest when they *reasonably believe* that an offence has been committed. In such cases, the officer can arrest anyone they reasonably suspect to have committed the offence.

In addition, the officer can only make an arrest when it is necessary for one of the reasons specified in section 24(5).

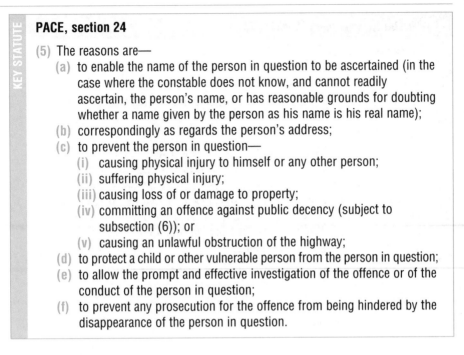

PACE, section 24

(5) The reasons are—

   (a) to enable the name of the person in question to be ascertained (in the case where the constable does not know, and cannot readily ascertain, the person's name, or has reasonable grounds for doubting whether a name given by the person as his name is his real name);

   (b) correspondingly as regards the person's address;

   (c) to prevent the person in question—

      (i) causing physical injury to himself or any other person;

      (ii) suffering physical injury;

      (iii) causing loss of or damage to property;

      (iv) committing an offence against public decency (subject to subsection (6)); or

      (v) causing an unlawful obstruction of the highway;

   (d) to protect a child or other vulnerable person from the person in question;

   (e) to allow the prompt and effective investigation of the offence or of the conduct of the person in question;

   (f) to prevent any prosecution for the offence from being hindered by the disappearance of the person in question.

Notification of arrest

Once arrested, a person should be immediately notified that they are under arrest and the reasons for the arrest. Failure to do so may render the arrest unlawful.

PACE, section 28

(1) where a person is arrested, otherwise than by being informed that he is under arrest, the arrest is not lawful unless the person arrested is informed that he is under arrest as soon as is practicable after his arrest.

(2) where a person is arrested by a constable, subsection (1) above applies regardless of whether the fact of the arrest is obvious.

(3) no arrest is lawful unless the person arrested is informed of the ground for the arrest at the time of, or as soon as is practicable after, the arrest.

Christie v. *Leachinsky* [1947] AC 573

Concerning: notification of arrest

Facts

Arresting officers failed to notify the arrested person of the reason for his arrest.

Legal principle

'It is a condition of lawful arrest that the party arrested should know on what charge or on suspicion of what crime he is arrested: and, therefore, just as a private person arresting on suspicion must acquaint the party with the cause of his arrest, so must a policeman arresting without warrant on suspicion state at the time (unless the party is already acquainted with it), on what charge the arrest is being made or at least inform him of the facts which are said to constitute a crime on his part.'

Caution

An arrested person must also be cautioned in the following terms on arrest and also when questioned:

PACE, Code of Practice C 10.5

'You do not have to say anything. But it may harm your defence if you do not mention when questioned something which you later rely on in Court. Anything you do say may be given in evidence.'

FURTHER THINKING

The wording of the caution emphasises that a suspect who does not mention information when questioned, but who later seeks to rely on that information as part of their defence in court may find the court drawing an 'adverse inference' from their failure to provide the information earlier (i.e. concluding that they are lying). This undermines the 'right to silence', which was seen as a fundamental right of the accused and was introduced by the Criminal Justice and Public Order Act 1994. This change was highly criticised and continues to cause argument and concern. See Leng (2001).

■ Search of premises

Search of premises can be either with or without warrant but, in both cases, can only be carried out by a police officer.

Search with warrant

KEY STATUTE

PACE, section 8(1)

If on an application made by a constable a justice of the peace is satisfied that there are reasonable grounds for believing—

(a) that [an indictable offence] has been committed; and
(b) that there is material on premises which is likely to be of substantial value (whether by itself or together with other material) to the investigation of the offence; and
(c) that the material is likely to be relevant evidence; and
(d) that it does not consist of or include items subject to legal privilege, excluded material or special procedure material.

He may issue a warrant authorising a constable to enter and search the premises.

Search without warrant

The police can enter and search premises without warrant under the following provisions of PACE:

PACE provision	When?
s. 17	To affect an arrest (i.e. enter premises to arrest a person and conduct a search when on the premises).
s. 18	To search premises 'occupied and controlled' by a person under arrest (i.e. once a person has been arrested, to visit and search their house).
s. 32	To search any premises where the arrested person was immediately prior to their arrest (i.e. where a person ran into a house immediately before being arrested and so may have concealed material there).

What can be seized?

KEY STATUTE

PACE, section 19(2), (3)

(2) The constable may seize anything which is on the premises if he has reasonable grounds for believing—

(a) that it has been obtained in consequence of the commission of an offence; and

(b) that it is necessary to seize it in order to prevent it being concealed, lost, damaged, altered or destroyed.

(3) The constable may seize anything which is on the premises if he has reasonable grounds for believing—

(a) that it is evidence in relation to an offence which he is investigating or any other offence; and

(b) that it is necessary to seize it in order to prevent the evidence being concealed, lost, altered or destroyed.

Problem area What can be seized?

Do not make the mistake of writing that the police can only seize property relating to the offence they are investigating. As you can see from section 19, once on the premises, they can seize material relating to *any* offence (even if they did not know about it when they entered the premises).

Detention and questioning

The other main area of police powers covers the detention and questioning of suspects. Examination questions usually centre on a number of key areas.

Detention before charge

A key question is how long a suspect can be held by the police without being charged. This period of detention is subject to regular review.

Up to (total maximum hours)	On the authority of
24 hours (subject to periodic review after first six hours and then every nine hours)	Custody Officer
36 hours	Senior Officer (Superintendent or above)
96 hours	Magistrate

Note that the above excludes terrorism cases, where the maximum detention period is currently 28 days.

Detention before charge

After being charged, the suspect should be brought before a magistrates' court 'as soon as practicable' (PACE, section 40).

Questioning

A suspect may only be questioned in the police station and under caution (see arrest). PACE also provides for confession evidence to be excluded from court if unfairly obtained.

KEY STATUTE

PACE, section 76(2)

If, in any proceedings where the prosecution proposes to give in evidence a confession made by an accused person, it is represented to the court that the confession was or may have been obtained—

(a) by oppression of the person who made it; or
(b) in consequence of anything said or done which was likely, in the circumstances existing at the time, to render unreliable any confession which might be made by him in consequence thereof,

the court shall not allow the confession to be given in evidence against him except in so far as the prosecution proves to the court beyond reasonable doubt that the confession (notwithstanding that it may be true) was not obtained as aforesaid.

Note that section 76 applies only to confession evidence. By contrast, section 78 applies to any form of unfairly obtained evidence.

KEY STATUTE

PACE, section 78

In any proceedings the court may refuse to allow evidence on which the prosecution proposes to rely to be given if it appears to the court that, having regard to all the circumstances, including the circumstances in which the evidence was obtained, the admission of the evidence would have such an adverse effect on the fairness of the proceedings that the court ought not to admit it.

Chapter Summary:
Putting it all together

TEST YOURSELF

☐ Can you tick all the points from the revision checklist at the beginning of this chapter?

☐ Take the **end-of-chapter quiz** on the companion website.

☐ Test your knowledge of the cases below with the **revision flashcards** on the website.

☐ Attempt the problem question from the beginning of the chapter using the guidelines below.

☐ Go to the companion website to try out other questions.

Answer guidelines

See the problem question at the start of the chapter.

Points to remember when answering this question
Consider in turn the stop search and the search of premises. In each case, the central question is whether the officers have acted in accordance with PACE.

With the stop search, do the officers have the reasonable suspicion required to justify the search? The suspect clearly does not match the description and appears to be stopped purely on the basis of his previous convictions – this is not sufficient.

The officers do not inform him of their station/names or the object and grounds for the search – another breach of PACE.

There is the question of whether the barred bus shelter is a place to which the public have access.

The officers find items which may be used to commit burglary (one of the specified offences for stop search) but this is 'after the event' – remember the officers should have reasonable grounds to justify the search, not perform the search to produce reasonable grounds.

With regard to the search of the flat, there is no mention of the suspect being under arrest, which is a requirement of sections 17, 18 and 32. Therefore, the search would be *prima facie* unlawful.

However, once on the premises, the officers can still seize the drugs and use this as the basis for an arrest.

Make your answer really stand out
Although the search of the flat appears to be unlawful, point out that the pragmatic approach of the courts towards obtaining evidence means that the search would not be challenged by the courts. This is in marked contrast to the USA, where such an illegal search would render any evidence inadmissible.

FURTHER READING

Jason-Lloyd, L. (2006) 'The New Powers of Arrest – Some Food for Thought', 160 *Criminal Law* 4–6.

Leng, R. (2001) 'Silence Pre-trial, Reasonable Expectations and the Normative Distortion of Fact-Finding', 5 *International Journal of Evidence and Proof* 240.

Newburn, T. and Reiner, R. (2004) 'From PC Dixon to Dixon plc: Policing and Police Powers Since 1954', *Criminal Law Review* 601–18.

Nicholson, D. (1992) 'The Citizen's Duty to Assist the Police', *Criminal Law Review* 611–22.

Ormerod, D. C. and Birch, D. (2004) 'The Evolution of the Discretionary Exclusion of Evidence', *Criminal Law Review* 767–88.

Ramage, S. (2006) 'The Revised Police PACE Codes of Practice: "An Englishman's Home was his Castle"', 159 *Criminal Law* 6–8.

The Brixton Disorders 10–12 April 1981: Report of an Inquiry (the Scarman Report) (1981) London: HMSO.

9
Judicial review

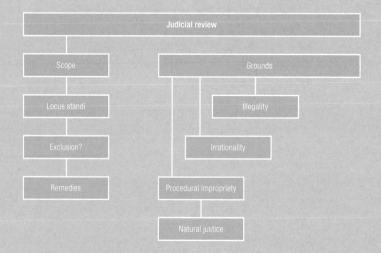

A printable version of this topic map is available from
www.pearsoned.co.uk/lawexpress

Revision Checklist

What you need to know:

- [ ] The role of judicial review as a mechanism for ensuring the accountability of the executive and as a safeguard against the misuse of delegated powers
- [ ] Decisions which are (and are not) subject to judicial review and assessing the requirements to bring an action
- [ ] The various grounds for judicial review
- [ ] Remedies
- [ ] The effectiveness of attempts to exclude judicial review

Introduction

Judicial review allows the individual to directly challenge at least some of the decision-making powers of the state.

There are relatively few mechanisms by which we can challenge the operation of the state; however, judicial review allows the courts to rule on the legality of decisions made by the state and, in some cases, overturn them. This is a powerful weapon for the individual, ensuring that those in power do not exceed their authority. For this reason, judicial review is an essential topic within any course on constitutional and administrative law and one which is almost certain to feature in examinations in some form or other.

Essay question advice

Essay questions on judicial review will ask you to consider the two essential elements of any law assessment – *description* and *analysis*. In this way, questions will ask you not only to set out what judicial review is (and the function which it performs within the constitution) but also how effective it is in fulfilling this role. Remember that mere description will never enable you to achieve the higher grades. These are reserved for answers which also display some critical analysis.

Problem questions on judicial review are very common and usually require you to consider one or more case studies to determine which, if any, of the grounds for judicial review may be applicable (together with their likely chances of success). As with all problem questions, the key to high marks is to adopt a methodical approach which deals with each element in turn, weighing up the competing arguments and producing a reasoned conclusion which offers at least some advice to the parties.

Sample question

Could you answer this question? Below is a typical problem question that could arise on this topic. Guidelines on answering the question are included at the end of this chapter, whilst a sample essay question and guidance on tackling it can be found on the companion website.

Problem question

Alisha applied to her local authority for a licence to serve alcohol at a new restaurant she was in the process of opening. Under the (fictitious) Restaurants Act 2000, a local Licensing Authority may refuse to issue an alcohol licence on grounds specified under section 33 of the Act.

The Licensing Authority meets every month but is also responsible for the licensing of pubs and gambling establishments and so is usually very busy. At the May meeting, the Authority did not have time to deal with Alisha's application and so delegated the task to a sub-committee, made up of three local people, David, Martin and Ian. On the day the sub-committee was supposed to meet to consider applications, David was called away to another meeting and Martin was ill. This left Ian, who made the decision himself not to grant the licence to Alisha.

On 1 June 2007, Alisha received a letter simply stating that her application had been refused. She was not told of the reasons why. She has also been informed that she will have to wait 12 months before she can make a new application.

Alisha has since found out that the restaurant over the road from hers has recently been bought by Ian.

Advise Alisha on whether she might be able to challenge the decision.

■ The operation of judicial review

It is important to recognise that judicial review fulfils a particular function within the constitution in allowing the individual to challenge decisions made by the state. Judicial review is relatively common and is used in relation to many different types of decisions, however not all decisions made by the state are subject to judicial review. Therefore, when attempting an examination question on the topic, the first point to be established is whether the particular decision is subject to judicial review.

The constitutional significance of judicial review

Judicial review is a mechanism to ensure the accountability of executive power within the constitution. As such, it allows the courts (under certain circumstances) to rule on the legality of how executive powers are exercised.

REVISION NOTE

Any discussion of the role of judicial review allows you to introduce references to a number of different aspects of constitutional law. For example, as judicial review is a mechanism for the judiciary to exert control over the executive, it can be viewed as part of the 'separation of powers'. Similarly, as judicial review is limited to secondary legislation (which is not debated in Parliament), it can be seen to provide a safeguard to ensure that such delegated powers are not misused.

Judicial review as a challenge to process

It is crucial to note that judicial review is a challenge to the process by which the decision was made, rather than the decision itself. The question is not whether the decision itself was correct, but whether the powers given to the decision-making body were used correctly.

Which decisions are susceptible to judicial review?

As stated previously, not all executive decisions are open to judicial review. To qualify, *all* of the following conditions must be satisfied:

The decision must be made by a public body

As a 'public law' remedy, judicial review is only available where the decision has been made by a public (rather than a private) body.

R v. Disciplinary Committee of the Jockey Club, ex parte Aga Khan [1993] 2 All ER 853

Concerning: availability of judicial review

Facts

A horse belonging to the Aga Khan was disqualified from a race by the Disciplinary Committee after failing a drugs test. The Aga Khan sought judicial review of the Committee's decision.

Legal principle

It was held that the Jockey Club was not a public body and, therefore, its decisions were not subject to judicial review. The relationship between the Club and its members was a matter for the private law.

R v. Panel on Take-overs and Mergers, ex parte Datafin plc [1987] QB 815

Concerning: availability of judicial review

Facts

The Panel was established by the City of London in order to regulate the takeover and merger of companies. Datafin sought judicial review of a panel decision to reject a complaint which it had made.

Legal principle

Given the public importance of its role, the Panel could be regarded as a 'public body' and so its decisions could be subject to judicial review.

The decision must be made under delegated powers

Remember the relationship between primary and secondary legislation in Chapter 5? The primary legislation (the Act of Parliament) can delegate powers to a person or body to implement secondary legislation (rules, regulations, codes of practice, etc.), which is why such provisions are also known as 'delegated legislation'. This is central to the operation of judicial review because only decisions made under such delegated powers are open to judicial review. Crucially, primary legislation – i.e. an Act of Parliament – is *not* subject to judicial review.

Bringing an action for judicial review

An action for judicial review is commenced in the High Court but requires permission (formerly known as the 'leave') of the court. In bringing an action, you must satisfy the court of two elements:

▌ The existence of a *prima facie* case (i.e. that there appears to be a case to answer).
▌ That the claimant has *locus standi* (i.e. the right to bring the case).

Locus standi

This simply means: do you (rather than someone else) have the right to bring this case? This is usually expressed in terms of having a 'sufficient interest' in the disputed matter. This is intended to prevent frivolous and time-wasting actions from so-called 'vexatious litigants'.

KEY CASE

R v. *Inland Revenue, ex parte National Federation of Self-employed and Small Businesses* **[1982] AC 617**

Concerning: *locus standi* for judicial review

Facts

The Federation sought to challenge the Inland Revenue's procedures for levying taxes on casual workers engaged by Fleet Street newspapers. The Federation argued that their members (who did not benefit from this arrangement) were, therefore, disadvantaged.

Legal principle

It was held by the House of Lords that, as the taxation arrangement did not apply to the individual members of the Federation, the Federation could not bring an action.

It may be possible, however, for a claimant to bring an action where they have no direct interest if there is a wider point of public interest to be decided by the action.

R v. HM Inspectorate of Pollution, ex parte Greenpeace (No. 2) [1994] 4 All ER 329

Concerning: *locus standi* for judicial review

Facts

The environmental campaign group, Greenpeace, sought to bring an action to challenge the policy of discharging toxic waste from the Sellafield nuclear plant into the Irish Sea.

Legal principle

It was held that, although Greenpeace clearly was not directly affected by the policy, the fact that it was an internationally recognised organisation, with access to resources and expertise, meant that it was much better equipped to bring an action than the actual residents affected by the policy.

Grounds for judicial review

An action must be brought on one or more 'grounds' (reasons), as set out in *Council of Civil Service Unions* v. *Minister for the Civil Service* (the 'GCHQ' case). There are only three grounds on which an action may be brought, but note that it is possible to argue that more than one of the grounds apply.

Council of Civil Service Unions v. *Minister for the Civil Service (the 'GCHQ Case')* [1985] AC 374

Concerning: the grounds for judicial review

Facts

It was decided by the government that workers at the secret Government Communications Headquarters (GCHQ) should not be allowed to join a trade union in case this led to them going on strike. The government altered, by means of prerogative power, the terms of employment of the workers to prohibit union membership. The union sought judicial review of the policy.

Legal principle

It was held by Lord Diplock that there were three grounds for judicial review: Illegality, irrationality and procedural impropriety.

Note that this case also appears in Chapter 2, as an example of how the courts have treated prerogative powers. Remember that the union sought to challenge the government's policy against union membership at GCHQ (implemented by prerogative power) by means of judicial review.

1. 'Illegality'

Although the first ground, 'illegality', would seem to suggest that the body which made the decision has acted against the law, it is better to see this in terms of a decision-maker who has acted *outside their authority*. In this way the decision is said to be *ultra vires* (beyond powers). This can be contrasted with a decision which is *intra vires* (within powers).

Problem area 'Illegality' and *Ultra Vires*

The concept of 'Illegality' can be a difficult one to grasp but is easier if you think of it in terms of 'absence of authority'. The manager of a shop has the power to make decisions about what happens in the shop, but cannot walk into the shop next door and issue orders – they have no authority to do so. In the same way, a decision-maker will be given powers to make decisions in a specific area; if they move outside that area, their decisions may be *ultra vires*.

KEY CASE

Attorney General v. *Fulham Corporation* [1921] 1 Ch 440

Concerning: illegality and *ultra vires*

Facts

The corporation had a statutory obligation (in an attempt to prevent disease) to provide washhouses for the poor, The authority sought to open a commercial laundry under this power.

Legal principle

It was held that the purpose of the power was to provide washing facilities for the very poorest people within the community. Opening a commercial laundry which would charge money to clean clothes was clearly not within the power and so was *ultra vires*.

KEY CASE

***R v. Richmond upon Thames London Borough Council, ex parte McCarthy & Stone (Developments) Ltd* [1992] 2 AC 48**

Concerning: illegality and *ultra vires*

Facts

The council was required to consider planning applications but also introduced a system of 'informal consultations', for which they charged £25.

Legal principle

The House of Lords held that, although the system of 'informal consultation' with applicants was helpful, there was no power to levy the £25 charge. Therefore, this was *ultra vires*.

Relevant and irrelevant considerations

A decision may be deemed *ultra vires* if it is made on the basis of factors which are irrelevant or, alternatively, if the decision-maker ignores factors which are relevant.

KEY CASE

***R v. Port Talbot Borough Council, ex parte Jones* [1988] 2 All ER 207**

Concerning: irrelevant considerations

Facts

A councillor was granted a tenancy on a council house ahead of the waiting list. The council justified the decision on the basis that the councillor needed to live within the borough she represented and needed a house to carry out her work for the council.

Legal principle

It was held that this was an irrelevant factor and so the decision was *ultra vires*. The council should base housing decisions on need and on the waiting list.

Unauthorised delegation of powers

Similarly, if the decision-making power is given to a specific body, they do not have the authority to delegate that decision-making power to another person. Under such circumstances, decisions made by the person who acts without authority are *ultra vires*.

KEY CASE

Barnard v. National Dock Labour Board [1953] 2 QB 18

Concerning: unauthorised delegation of powers

Facts

The National Board had the power to discipline its members but delegated this power to port managers.

Legal principle

It was held that the delegation was unlawful and so any disciplinary powers exercised by the port managers were *ultra vires*.

2. 'Irrationality'

The second ground, 'irrationality', is often described in terms of 'unreasonableness', which is defined in accordance with the decision in *Associated Provincial Picture Houses Ltd* v. *Wednesbury Corporation* (1948).

Associated Provincial Picture Houses Ltd v. *Wednesbury Corporation* [1948] 1 KB 223

Concerning: the reasonableness of a decision

Facts

The local authority had the power to license cinemas to open on Sundays, subject to whatever conditions it thought fit to impose. In considering this application, the authority decided that no person under 15 years should be admitted on a Sunday. The company challenged this decision as unreasonable.

Legal principle

It was held that a decision would not be unreasonable if it was not 'so unreasonable that no reasonable authority could ever have come to it'.

Problem area *Wednesbury* unreasonableness

At first glance, the test for '*Wednesbury* unreasonableness' might appear somewhat confusing. All it means is that, if a reasonable authority *could* (not *would*) have come to this decision, then it is reasonable. As you can see, this is a fairly broad category and so makes it more likely than not that the decision will be seen as reasonable. However, it is still quite possible for a decision to be held unreasonable depending on the individual circumstances.

R v. Secretary of State for the Home Department, ex parte Brind [1991] 1 AC 696

Concerning: unreasonableness

Facts

The government introduced a ban on the TV transmission of any speech by the IRA or Sinn Fein.

Legal principle

It was held that this was not so unreasonable that no reasonable Home Secretary could ever have reached the decision. Therefore, the ban was not unreasonable.

Hall and Co Ltd v. Shoreham-by-Sea Urban Development Corporation [1964] 1 All ER 1

Concerning: unreasonableness

Facts

Hall & Co were granted planning permission to develop their land but subject to a condition that they construct, at their own expense, a road to be used by the owners of neighbouring land and the general public.

Legal principle

It was held that this was an unreasonable condition, as it passed the public burden of constructing roads to the individual.

FURTHER THINKING

A related area has been the development of 'proportionality' as a consideration in judicial review – i.e. whether the action proposed was no more than was absolutely necessary to address the problem. This is a concept from European law and has become particularly significant in relation to the implementation of EU provisions and issues of human rights under the Convention on Human Rights. For discussion of the principle in recent domestic cases, see Qureshi (2007).

3. Procedural impropriety

The third ground, procedural impropriety, has the benefit of being the easiest to recognise. As the name suggests, the basic question is: 'has the correct procedure been followed?' If not, then the decision may be called into question. This is intended to ensure that decision-making bodies follow the necessary steps in reaching their decisions.

Problem area Questioning a decision for procedural impropriety

Note that the fact that the correct procedure was not followed does not automatically mean that the decision itself is wrong, merely that there *may* have been a different outcome. This is in keeping with the general purpose of judicial review, which looks to the way in which the decision was made.

KEY CASE

Agricultural, Horticultural and Forestry Industry Training Board v. *Aylesbury Mushrooms Ltd* [1972] 1 All ER 280

Concerning: the nature of procedural impropriety

Facts

The minister was empowered to establish Industrial Training Boards but, in doing so, was required to consult relevant organisations in the area concerned. The AHFITB was set up without such consultation.

Legal principle

It was held that the failure to engage in the required consultation invalidated the establishment of the board.

KEY CASE

Vale of Glamorgan Borough Council v. *Palmer and Bowles* [1983] Crim LR 334

Concerning: the nature of procedural impropriety

Facts

The council were empowered to issue tree preservation orders to protect selected trees within the borough. Each order required a plan identifying the relevant tree to be available for public inspection. In this particular case, no such plan was made available.

Legal principle

It was held that the failure to follow the procedure rendered the order invalid.

Natural justice

Within procedural impropriety there is also a ground for judicial review known as 'natural justice' – i.e. decisions which contravene basic principles of fairness. These include the rule against bias (*nemo judex in causa sua*) and the right to a fair hearing (*audi alteram partem*).

KEY CASE

Dimes v. Grand Junction Canal (1852) 3 HL Cas 759

Concerning: bias

Facts

The Lord Chancellor heard a case involving the Grand Junction Canal Company and found in their favour. It later emerged that he held a shareholding in the company.

Legal principle

It was held that the shareholding raised the question of bias and so invalidated the decision.

KEY CASE

R v. Bow Street Metropolitan Stipendary Magistrates' Court, ex parte Pinochet Ugarte (No. 2) [2000] 1 AC 119

Concerning: bias

Facts

Former dictator Augusto Pinochet was arrested during a visit to London pending an extradition request from the Spanish government, which wanted him to stand trial for alleged war crimes. The House of Lords was required to consider whether a former head of state enjoyed immunity from extradition.

Legal principle

The House of Lords held that Pinochet did not have immunity, however it emerged that one of the Law Lords had close links with Amnesty International, which was pressing for the extradition to take place. This raised the possibility of bias and so required the decision to be set aside and the case reheard.

EXAM TIP

Be sure to point out that there is no need to show that there is bias in such cases. All that is necessary is the *possibility* or the *appearance* of bias – this is sufficient to have the decision set aside.

Ridge v. Baldwin [1964] AC 40

Concerning: right to a fair hearing

Facts

R was Chief Constable of Brighton and was charged with conspiracy. He was cleared but the trial judge was highly critical of his leadership. Following the judge's comments, R was dismissed without a hearing or being allowed to present his case.

Legal principle

It was held that the right to a fair hearing required a person to be afforded the opportunity to present their case.

Is there a right to be informed of the reasons for the decision?

There is also the question of whether the decision-maker is required to state the reasons for the decision. Although there is no general common law duty requiring reasons to be given, the general trend is towards explaining why the decision was made.

R v. Secretary of State for the Home Department, ex parte Doody [1994] 1 AC 531

Concerning: the requirement to provide reasons for decisions

Facts

The applicants were life sentence prisoners whose applications for parole were refused without any reasons being given. They sought disclosure of the reasoning behind the decision.

Legal principle

It was held that, although there remained no general duty to disclose the reasons for decisions, this was contrary to the public interest in such serious matters. Also, where a decision was amenable to judicial review, it was necessary for the applicant to know the reasoning employed by the decision maker in order to prepare their case.

■Remedies

When answering a question on judicial review, you should always mention the possible remedies available. Note that the names for some of the remedies have changed (the old titles are included in brackets in the table below).

Remedies	Effect
Quashing order (certiorari)	Overturns the original decision.
Mandatory order (mandamus)	Compels the decision-maker to act in a certain way.
Prohibiting order (prohibition)	Prevents the decision-maker from making a decision which would later be subject to a quashing order.
Injunction	Can be either positive (compelling action) or negative (prohibiting action). As such, they are very much like quashing orders and mandatory orders but can be also be made on an interim (temporary) basis, pending the outcome of the case.
Declaration	A judicial statement of the legal position of the parties.

■Attempts to exclude judicial review

Often (and understandably), decision-makers would like to remove the possibility of their decisions being challenged by judicial review. However, as a constitutional safeguard, this is not generally seen as desirable. The most obvious way of trying to remove the possibility of judicial review is to exclude such powers in the statute which delegates the decision-making power by means of an 'ouster clause'. Despite such statutory attempts to restrict judicial review, the courts have usually succeeded in adopting an interpretation which permits challenges to continue.

REVISION NOTE
Note that the operation of judicial review can raise a number of the constitutional doctrines outlined in Chapter 3. The judiciary exerting control over the executive by means of judicial review raises aspects of the separation of powers and attempts by Parliament to exclude judicial review by means of statutory provisions illustrates aspects of parliamentary sovereignty. Make sure to mention that you are aware of this in your discussion of judicial review.

KEY STATUTE

Foreign Compensation Act 1950, section 4

Determinations of the Compensation Commission shall not be called into question in any court of law.

(Note: this provision was later removed by the Statute Law (Repeals) Act 1989.)

KEY CASES

Anisminic Ltd v. *Foreign Compensation Commission* **[1969] 1 All ER 208**

Concerning: ouster clauses

Facts

The claimants sought to challenge a determination of the Compensation Commission. The Commission sought to rely on section 4 of the Foreign Compensation Act 1950.

Legal principle

It was held that the word 'determination' did not exclude the court's power to consider whether the decision was correct *in law* (remembering the difference between judicial review and an appeal).

Chapter Summary:
Putting it all together

TEST YOURSELF

☐ Can you tick all the points from the revision checklist at the beginning of this chapter?

☐ Take the **end-of-chapter quiz** on the companion website.

☐ Test your knowledge of the cases below with the **revision flashcards** on the website.

☐ Attempt the problem question from the beginning of the chapter using the guidelines below.

☐ Go to the companion website to try out other questions.

Answer guidelines

See the problem question at the start of the chapter.

Points to remember when answering this question
The delegation of the power to consider applications to the sub-committee may be an unauthorised delegation.

Is the 'one man' committee sufficient – does the committee require a certain number of people to make valid decisions? You do not have this information, but it is an important point to raise as requiring further clarification.

Possibility of bias, given Gordon's purchase of the competing restaurant. This suggests grounds of procedural impropriety, which may also extend to the 'single member' committee and possibly 'natural justice' (bias).

No reasons given for the decision.

Make your answer really stand out
Mention the absence of a common law duty to provide reasons for the decision but emphasise the increasing expectation that reasons will be given.

Remember to emphasise that the mere appearance of bias may be sufficient to overturn the decision.

Do not ignore the issue of possible remedies. Here the most probable outcome is a quashing order.

FURTHER READING

Craig, P. (1999) 'Competing Models of Judicial Review', *Public Law* 428–47.
Craig, P. (2001) 'Constitutional Analysis, Constitutional Principle and Judicial Review'. *Public Law* 763–80.
Jowell, J. (1999) 'Of Vires and Vacuums: The Constitutional Context of Judicial Review', *Public Law* 448–60.
Qureshi, K. (2007) 'Under Review', 157 *New Law Journal* 315.
Tremblay, L. (2003) 'General Legitimacy of Judicial Review and the Fundamental Basis of Constitutional Law', 23 *Oxford Journal of Legal Studies* 525.
Tremblay, L. (2005) 'The Legitimacy of Judicial Review: The Limits of Dialogue Between Courts and Legislature', 3 *International Journal of Constitutional Law* 617.
Woolf, H. (1998) 'Judicial Review: The Tensions Between the Executive and the Judiciary', 114 *Law Quarterly Review* 579–93.

10
Tribunals, inquiries and ombudsmen

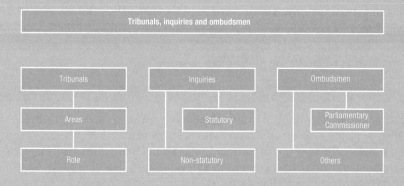

A printable version of this topic map is available from
www.pearsoned.co.uk/lawexpress

Revision Checklist

What you need to know:

- [ ] The range of work undertaken by tribunals and their powers
- [ ] The function and composition of public inquiries
- [ ] The role of the Parliamentary Commissioner
- [ ] The range of work undertaken by ombudsmen

Introduction:

Not all matters are settled in the courts – there are a range of other mechanisms available.

Although we tend to think of the courts as the place where disputes are settled, constitutional law has given us a range of alternatives, often under the justification of speed and cost. Tribunals operate in a number of areas and provide relatively speedy and informal decisions. The same cannot be said of inquiries, however, which can be incredibly lengthy and expensive. A third mechanism, the ombudsman, is a relatively recent development. All three processes must be considered and their relative advantages and disadvantages understood.

Essay question advice

Essay questions may ask you to consider the role played by such alternatives to traditional litigation and their effectiveness in terms of constitutional accountability. This requires a clear understanding of the relative merits of each mechanism and the ability to engage in a rounded analysis which places them within the broader constitutional context.

Problem question advice

A problem question may require you to consider a particular scenario or series of scenarios and allocate them to the appropriate forum (e.g. tribunal or ombudsman). Again, the question will require you to demonstrate that you understand the advantages and disadvantages of the various mechanisms.

Sample question

Could you answer this question? Below is a typical essay question that could arise on this topic. Guidelines on answering the question are included at the end of this chapter, whilst a sample problem question and guidance on tackling it can be found on the companion website.

'Tribunals, inquiries and ombudsmen make a valuable contribution to ensuring the accountability of the state.'

Discuss.

■Tribunals

Tribunals operate in many areas of law, where they are designed to settle disputes but without the formality, time and cost of litigation. Most act to hear appeals from decision-making bodies or committees. The Council on Tribunals suggests that tribunals:

■ are accessible to all;
■ are quick, informal, and as cheap as possible;
■ provide the right to an oral hearing in public;
■ give reasons for their decisions;
■ are seen to be independent, impartial and fair to all.

Types of tribunal

There are numerous tribunals covering a wide range of administration and decision-making. Examples include:

Tribunal	Cases heard
Asylum and Immigration Tribunal	Appeals against immigration decisions.
Criminal Injuries Compensation Appeals Panel	Appeals against decisions by the Criminal Injuries Compensation Authority.
Employment Tribunal	Disputes between employers and employees.
Employment Appeal Tribunal	Appeals from the Employment Tribunal.
Lands Tribunal	Disputes surrounding compensation following the compulsory purchase of land.
Mental Health Review Tribunal	Appeals against detention under the Mental Health Act.

Advantages and disadvantages of tribunals

Advantages	Disadvantages
Speed – tribunals are generally much quicker than courts.	Credibility – may be seen as lacking the 'weight' of a court.
Informality – there is an emphasis on less formal language, procedure, rules of evidence, etc.	Increasing formality – as cases become more complex the emphasis on informality may be sacrificed.
Cost – even if legal representation is used, the quicker proceedings mean less cost.	Increasing representation – applicants may still choose to instruct legal representatives, thereby undermining cost benefits.
Expertise – tribunals are usually staffed by experts in the field and focus on a narrow range of cases.	

FURTHER THINKING

The creation of the Tribunals Service brought tribunals under the supervision of a single body. This was in response to the Leggatt Review of 2000. For a discussion of the background and implications of this development, see Langdon-Down (2003).

■ Public inquiries

If tribunals are intended to be an informal and (relatively) inexpensive means of achieving justice, the same cannot be said for public inquiries, which can be lengthy and very expensive.

Types of inquiry

Inquires can be divided into two categories: statutory and non-statutory inquiries.

Statutory inquiries

The power to hold inquiries may be provided for in an Act of Parliament.

Town and Country Planning Act 1990, section 20

(1) Before deciding whether or not to approve a plan or part of a plan submitted to him under section 18(1), the Secretary of State shall consider any objection to it so far as made in accordance with the regulations.

(2) Where the whole or part of Part II of a unitary development plan is submitted to the Secretary of State under section 18(1) (whether or not the whole or part of Part I is also submitted), then, if any objections have been made to the plan or the relevant part of it as mentioned in subsection (1), before deciding whether to approve it he shall cause a local inquiry or other hearing to be held for the purpose of considering those objections.

Non-statutory inquiries

The other type of inquiry is set up on an individual basis to examine matters of widespread public concern. Usually, these are events such as disasters involving loss of life or national scandals. In each case the inquiry is established by the government under the chairmanship of a senior judge to investigate matters and restore public confidence by producing a definitive account of the facts.

Recent public inquiries	Subject
Hutton Inquiry (2004)	Death of Dr David Kelly and Iraq Intelligence
Saville Inquiry (opened 1998)	1972 'Bloody Sunday' shootings
Cullen Inquiry (1996)	Dunblane School shootings
Taylor Inquiry (1989)	Hillsborough disaster

Advantages and disadvantages of public inquiries

Advantages	Disadvantages
Depth – issues are examined in minute detail.	Time – inquiries often take years to assemble evidence and produce reports.
Scope – evidence is taken from all relevant parties and experts in the field.	Cost – as an example, the cost of the 'Bloody Sunday' Inquiry is currently estimated at £172 million.
Independence – chaired by a senior judge, the inquiry is independent of government.	Whitewash? – reports may face criticism if they are seen as reluctant to apportion blame.
Findings – Inquiries can seek to prevent further disasters by making recommendations and apportioning blame.	
Public confidence – inquiries often serve to restore public confidence.	

■ Ombudsmen

The third major mechanism for accountability is the most recently introduced. The concept of ombudsmen (individuals who would examine the use of government powers as they impact on the individual citizen) was introduced into the UK from Scandinavia in the 1960s. Now there are a number of such ombudsmen in both the public and private sectors. They are often titled 'Commissioner.'

The Parliamentary Commissioner for Administration

The Parliamentary Commissioner investigates complaints received from members of the public. The ombudsman investigates allegations of 'injustice in consequence of maladministration' by government departments.

The 'MP filter'

Although complaints come from members of the public, they must be referred to the Commissioner by an MP and this 'MP filter' has been criticised as acting as a deterrent to genuine complainants. However, suggestions that members of the public should be able to complain to the Commissioner directly have not yet been adopted.

Other ombudsmen

Health Service Commissioner	Investigates complaints about NHS trusts.
Local Government Commissioner	Investigates complaints surrounding the operation of local government.
Legal Services Commissioner	Investigates complaints surrounding the provision of legal services in England and Wales.

Advantages and disadvantages of ombudsmen

Advantages	Disadvantages
Independent – not aligned to government and so able to safeguard the individual.	'MP filter' – in relation to the Parliamentary Ombudsman, the requirement for complaints to be received via an MP can prevent legitimate complaints from being investigated.
Access – in a position to obtain the relevant information to investigate complaints thoroughly.	
Influence – can bring about wide-ranging changes to procedure.	Time – investigations may be slow moving.
	Power? – findings may not be binding on those involved

Chapter Summary:
Putting it all together

- [ ] Can you tick all the points from the revision checklist at the beginning of this chapter?
- [ ] Take the **end-of-chapter quiz** on the companion website.
- [ ] Test your knowledge of the cases below with the **revision flashcards** on the website.
- [ ] Attempt the essay question from the beginning of the chapter using the guidelines below.
- [ ] Go to the companion website to try out other questions.

Answer guidelines

See the essay question at the start of the chapter.

Points to remember when answering this question
Outline the nature of state power and the vital importance of mechanisms of accountability.

Approach each mechanism in turn, explaining what it is designed to achieve and the circumstances in which it is appropriate.

List the advantages and disadvantages of each mechanism, reflecting on how well each appears to achieve its stated objective.

Make your answer really stand out
Take the opportunity to include reference to other mechanisms for state accountability, most notably judicial review. Although this is not the subject of the question, a relatively brief mention will emphasise to the examiner that you see the role of tribunals, inquiries and ombudsmen within a broader context.

Always utilise examples to support your arguments.

Editorial (2006) 'Reform of Public Service Ombudsman', *Journal of Planning and Environmental Law* 623.
Kirkham, R. (2005) 'Auditing by Stealth? Special Reports and the Ombudsman', *Public Law* 740–48.

Langdon-Down, G. (2003) 'The Future of Tribunals: A Fair Hearing', 100.05 *Law Society Gazette* 21.

Nobles, R. (2001) 'Keeping Ombudsmen in Their Place', *Public Law* 308–28.

Quane, H. (2007) 'Challenging the Report of an Independent Inquiry under the Human Rights Act', *Public Law* 529–44.

Seneviratne, M. (2006) 'A New Ombudsman for Wales', *Public Law* 6–14.

Steele, I. (2004) 'Judging Judicial Inquiries', *Public Law* 738–49.

And finally, before the exam . . .

■Linking it all up

Traditionally, examination questions in constitutional and administrative law tend to concentrate on a single area, rather than combining a number of topics within the same question. However, it is in the nature of the subject that a question on one topic may include reference to another and being able to exploit this within the examination can help you to achieve higher grades. The examiner will want to see that you can approach the subject, not as a series of separate areas, but as a whole, pointing out where there is an overlap between different aspects of the state. This is particularly common in relation to aspects of the constitution such as the 'constitutional doctrines' of parliamentary sovereignty, the separation of powers and (to a lesser extent) the rule of law. The doctrines impact on all aspects of the operation of the constitution and so questions on topics as diverse as constitutional conventions, royal prerogative, police powers, civil liberties or judicial review should all be answered with some reference to the doctrines of the separation of powers and parliamentary sovereignty.

Question

Nathan and his friends are opposed to the government's foreign policy, particularly in relation to the Middle East. On Monday, Nathan learns that the Prime Minister will be visiting the Town Hall the next day to launch a new initiative to help the unemployed. Nathan quickly phones his friends and organises a protest march to coincide with the visit.

The following day, Nathan and his friends assemble around the corner from the Town Hall and begin to march, chanting anti-government slogans. However, the police, who are there in force, quickly arrest them. At the local police station, Nathan is not allowed to see a solicitor and is beaten by two police officers until he signs a 'confession' admitting to a conspiracy to kill the Prime Minister.

When he appears in court, the case against Nathan quickly collapses due to lack of evidence and Nathan argues that his human rights have been infringed. The trial judge comments that there may well have been a breach of Nathan's right to a fair trial under Article 6 of the European Convention, but adjourns the case for two months to allow the police to prepare their defence. The case attracts a lot of publicity and features on the evening news as a potential embarrassment for the police and the government.

The following week, the judge receives a telephone call from an official at the Home Office. He is told that the Home Secretary thinks that the judge 'would be sensible' to dismiss the case if he wants his career in the judiciary to continue. Outraged, the judge reveals the details of this conversation to the press and there are calls for the Home Secretary to resign. The Home Secretary flatly refuses to resign and indicates that he is prepared to use the royal prerogative to overturn the Human Rights Act 1998 in this case.

Points to remember when answering this question

The protesters have not complied with section 11 of the Public Order Act 1986 by giving written notice to the police six clear days prior to the procession.

Nathan's treatment at the police station clearly breaches the provisions of the Police and Criminal Evidence Act 1984 and its Codes of Practice, particularly Code C, covering detention and questioning. He should be allowed access to a solicitor and the circumstances in which his 'confession' is obtained make it likely that it would be excluded as evidence under section 76 and/or section 78 of PACE.

Nathan's right to a fair trial under Article 6 of the European Convention on Human Rights may have been infringed. Under section 6 of the Human Rights Act 1998, 'public authorities' are prohibited from acting in a way which is incompatible with Convention rights. Both the police and the court would qualify as 'public authorities' for the purposes of the 1998 Act.

The telephone call from the Home Office official raises the question of the separation of powers and the executive encroaching on the role of the judiciary.

The call also raises the convention of ministerial responsibility, as the Home Secretary should take responsibility for the actions of his official, particularly as it appears that the Home Secretary was aware of the call.

The threat by the Home Secretary to overrule the Human Rights Act by means of the royal prerogative requires consideration of the scope of prerogative powers. Following *Attorney General* v. *De Keyer's Royal Hotel*, statute will always prevail over prerogative power. This raises the question of parliamentary sovereignty and the accepted principle that an Act of Parliament will always take precedence over unwritten, historical powers such as the prerogative.

TEST YOURSELF

☐ Look at the revision checklists at the start of each chapter. Are you happy that you can now tick them all? If not, go back to the particular chapter and work through the material again. If you are still struggling, **seek help** from your tutor.

☐ Go to the companion website and revisit the interactive **quizzes** provided for each chapter.

☐ Make sure you can recall the **legal principles** of the key cases and statutes which you have revised.

☐ Go to the companion website and test your knowledge of cases and terms with the **revision flashcards.**

The constitution

The state

Institutions	Doctrines	and the individual

Civil liberties

Police powers	Freedom of speech	Freedom of assembly	Human rights

Other protections

Judicial review	Ombudsmen

A printable version of this subject map is available from
www.pearsoned.co.uk/lawexpress.

Glossary of terms

The glossary is divided into two parts: **key definitions** and **other useful terms**.

The **key definitions** can be found within relevant chapters as well as at the end of the book. These are the essential terms that you must know and understand in order to prepare for an examination or a piece of coursework.

The **other useful terms** provide definitions of other terms and phrases which you will encounter in this subject and may have forgotten the meaning of. These terms are highlighted in the text as they occur but the definition can only be found here.

Key definitions

Constitution	The framework of rules which dictate the way in which power is divided between the various parts of the state and the relationship between the state and the individual
Devolution	The process by which power is given (or 'devolved') from Westminster to Scotland, Wales and Northern Ireland, giving them greater control over their own affairs and the power to make their own laws in certain areas. This is not full independence, however, as Westminster retains power over key areas such as defence
Federal constitution	A constitution which has a division of powers between the central government and the government of individual states or regions
Monarchical constitution	A constitution based on the historical power of a Monarch who acts as head of state and in whose name power is exercised by the government
Republican constitution	A constitution with an elected president as the head of state who exercises power in the name of the state
Rights	There is no single definition of the term 'rights', but a number of legal theorists have suggested possible meanings of the word. One of the most commonly cited definitions comes from Wesley Hohfeld, who divided rights into

'Privileges', 'Claims', 'Powers' and 'Immunities'. The sorts of civil liberties which we normally think of when discussing rights would fall into Hohfeld's definition of a 'Claim' right – we have a claim against the state to uphold our 'rights'

Royal prerogative

This was defined by Dicey as 'the residue of discretionary or arbitrary authority .. legally left in the Hands of the Crown ... the remaining portion of the Crown's original authority'

Unitary constitution

A constitution with power concentrated in central government. Local government may exist but not with the constitutional status of the States under a federal constitution

Other useful terms

Absolute privilege	Immunity from legal action which is automatic and complete
Constitutional convention	An unwritten customary rule which dictates how the state will operate in certain circumstances
Executive	A body which both formulates and implements policies. In constitutional law this term is usually taken to mean the Cabinet
Judiciary	The courts. In constitutional law this term is usually reserved for the higher courts (i.e. the House of Lords)
Legislature	The body which makes legislation – i.e. Parliament
Ombudsman	Individual empowered to hear complaints about a particular aspect of the operation of the state
Parliamentary privilege	The collective rights of Parliament as an institution and the individual rights enjoyed by Members of Parliament
Parliamentary sovereignty	The principle that Parliament is the most powerful of the organs of state and can overrule the executive and the judiciary
Primary legislation	Acts of Parliament
Qualified privilege	Immunity from legal action which is not automatic and which depends on certain criteria being fulfilled
Rule of law	The principle that the law of the land applies equally to all
Secondary legislation	Statutory Instruments, Codes of Practice
Select committee	Committee of Parliament which considers the work of a particular Government department (e.g. Home Affairs Select Committee)
Separation of powers	Constitutional doctrine which divides powers between the various organs of state to prevent abuse
Standing committee	Committee of Parliament which considers Bills as they pass through the legislative process during the 'Committee stage' of approval.

Index